Social Studies

Daily Practice Workbook

20 weeks of fun activities

History • **Civics and Government** • **Geography** • **Economics**

ArgoPrep is one of the leading providers of supplemental educational products and services. We offer affordable and effective test prep solutions to educators, parents and students. Learning should be fun and easy! To access more resources visit us at www.argoprep.com.

Our goal is to make your life easier, so let us know how we can help you by e-mailing us at: info@argoprep.com.

- ArgoPrep is a recipient of the prestigious **Mom's Choice Award**.

- ArgoPrep also received the 2019 **Seal of Approval** from Homeschool.com for our award-winning workbooks.

- ArgoPrep was awarded the 2019 **National Parenting Products Award**, **Gold Medal Parent's Choice Award** and **the Tillywig Brain Child Award.**

SOCIAL STUDIES

Social Studies Daily Practice Workbook by ArgoPrep allows students to build foundational skills and review concepts. Our workbooks explore social studies topics in depth with ArgoPrep's 5 E's to build social studies mastery.

OTHER BOOKS BY ARGOPREP

Here are some other test prep workbooks by ArgoPrep you may be interested in. All of our workbooks come equipped with detailed video explanations to make your learning experience a breeze! Visit us at **www.argoprep.com**

COMMON CORE MATH SERIES

COMMON CORE ELA SERIES

INTRODUCING MATH!

Introducing Math! by ArgoPrep is an award-winning series created by certified teachers to provide students with high-quality practice problems. Our workbooks include topic overviews with instruction, practice questions, answer explanations along with digital access to video explanations. Practice in confidence - with ArgoPrep!

SCIENCE SERIES

Science Daily Practice Workbook by ArgoPrep is an award-winning series created by certified science teachers to help build mastery of foundational science skills. Our workbooks explore science topics in depth with ArgoPrep's 5 E'S to build science mastery.

KIDS SUMMER ACADEMY SERIES

ArgoPrep's Kids Summer Academy series helps prevent summer learning loss and gets students ready for their new school year by reinforcing core foundations in math, english and science. Our workbooks also introduce new concepts so students can get a head start and be on top of their game for the new school year!

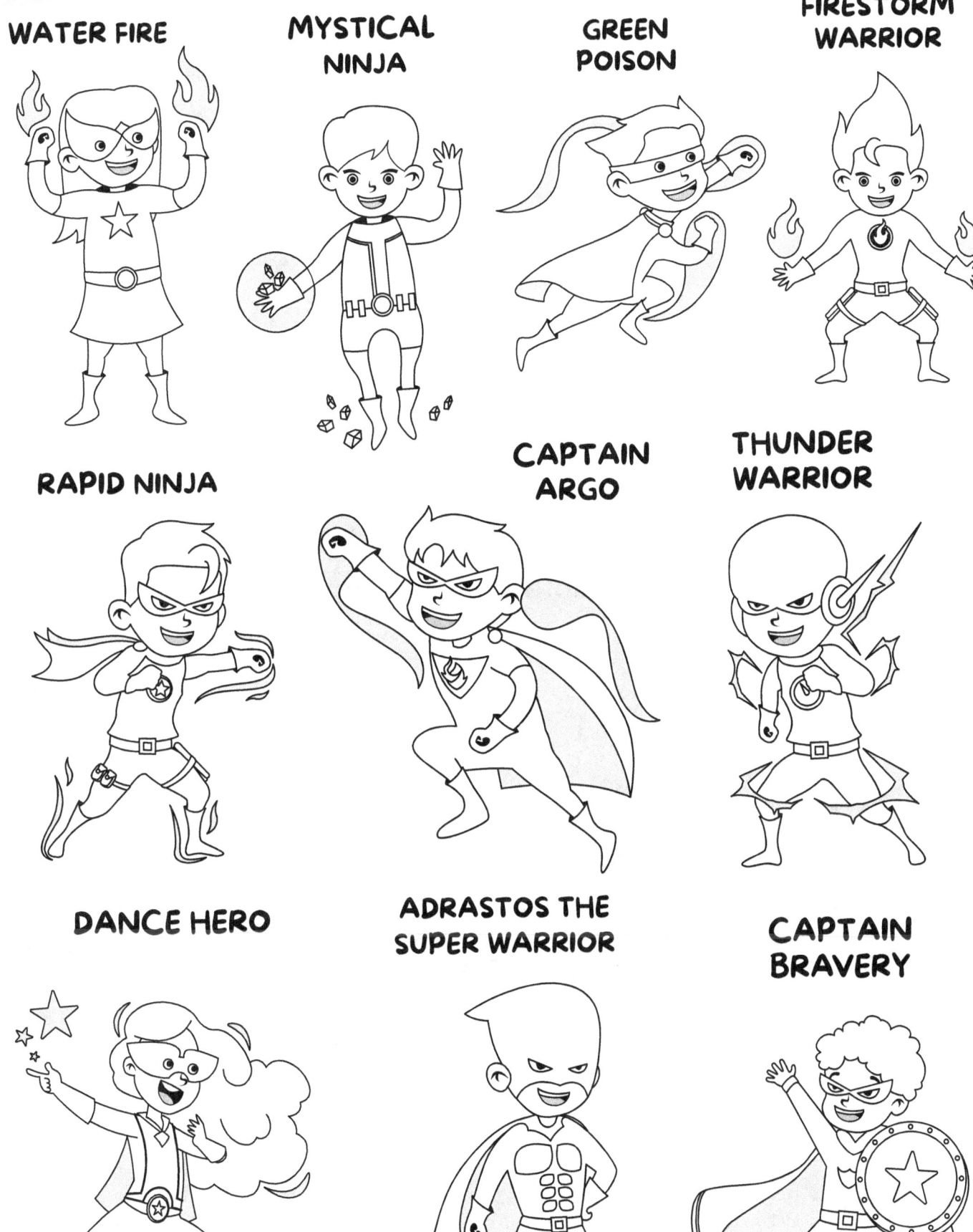

WATER FIRE

MYSTICAL
NINJA

GREEN
POISON

FIRESTORM
WARRIOR

RAPID NINJA

CAPTAIN
ARGO

THUNDER
WARRIOR

DANCE HERO

ADRASTOS THE
SUPER WARRIOR

CAPTAIN
BRAVERY

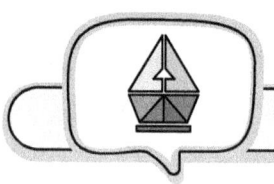
Introduction

Welcome to our eighth grade social studies workbook!

This workbook has been specifically designed to help students build mastery of foundational social studies skills that are taught in eighth grade. Included are 20 weeks of comprehensive instruction covering the four branches of social studies: History, Economics, Civics and Government, and Geography.

Students in 8th grade start with the time period of Reconstruction and learn more in detail about how the United States tried to heal from the wounds of the Civil War. This workbook follows the timeline in chronological order where students will work through topics such as Immigration, American Imperialism, The Roaring Twenties, World War II, The Cold War, and Post-War America.

At the conclusion of the 20 weeks of instruction, students should have a solid grasp of the concepts required by the National Council for Social Studies for eighth grade.

Table of Contents

How to Use the Book

All 20 weeks of daily activity pages in this book follow the same weekly structure. Students will work through each week with ArgoPrep's 5 E's to build mastery on the topic: **Engaging, Exploring, Explaining, Experiencing,** and **Elaborating** on the topic.

The activities in each of the sections align to the recommendations of the National Council for the Social Studies which will help prepare students for state standardized assessments. While the sections can be completed in any order, it is important to complete each week within the section in chronological order since the skills often build upon one another.

Each week focuses on one specific topic within the section. More information about the weekly structure can be found in the Weekly Planner section. This workbook also comes included with detailed video explanations which you can find on our website at argoprep.com/social8.

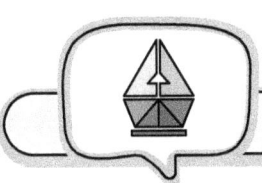
Weekly Planner

Day	Activity	Description
1	Engaging with the Topic	Read a short text on the topic and answer multiple choice questions.
2	Exploring the Topic	Interact with the topic on a deeper level by collecting, analyzing, and interpreting information.
3	Explaining the Topic	Make sense of the topic by explaining and beginning to draw conclusions about information.
4	Experiencing the Topic	Investigate the topic by making real-life connections.
5	Elaborating on the Topic	Reflect on the topic and use all information learned to draw conclusions and evaluate results.

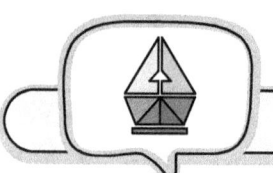
List of Topics

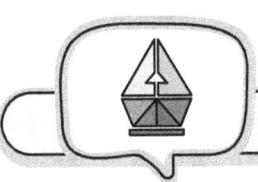
How to access video explanations?

Go to **argoprep.com/social8**
OR scan the QR Code:

WEEK 1

History
Reconstruction

This week, you will learn about Reconstruction, which was the period from 1865 to 1877 in which the United States tried to rebuild itself after the devastation of the Civil War.

ARGOPREP

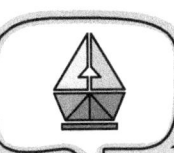
Directions: Read the text below. Then answer the questions that follow.

> When the Civil War ended in 1865, the United States entered a period called **Reconstruction**. This period, from 1865 to 1877, was an era in which the United States tried to heal from the wounds of war. There were three major plans for Reconstruction. The first was proposed by President Abraham Lincoln who in 1863 offered that if ten percent of voters swore allegiance to the United States then that state was eligible to reenter the Union. His plan gave more power to the individual states.
>
> Lincoln was assassinated in 1865 and replaced by his Vice President, Andrew Johnson. Johnson's plan, known as **Presidential Reconstruction**, offered amnesty and the return of all property (except formerly enslaved people) to most Confederates who swore an oath of allegiance to the Union.
>
> Both Lincoln and Johnson's plans were rejected by Congress which was controlled by the Republican Party. These Congress members, known as the **Radical Republicans**, feared the plans were too easy on the South since they would return to power the people who had been in charge of the South before the war. They worried that formerly enslaved people, called the freedmen, would be oppressed. They also thought the South should be punished.
>
> The Radical Republicans pushed through their own plan which restricted former Confederates from holding office. They also funded education for freedmen, established military occupation throughout the South, and supported civil rights for African Americans. The leading laws of this plan were the Fourteenth and Fifteenth Amendments to the Constitution. The **Fourteenth Amendment** guaranteed equal protection under the law to all citizens, including former enslaved people. The **Fifteenth Amendment** guaranteed the right to vote to all males of any "race, color, or previous condition of servitude."

1. What did the Fourteenth Amendment do?

    A. ended slavery in Confederate states

    B. gave the right to vote to formerly enslaved people

    C. provided the same justice to people of all races

    D. gave amnesty to Confederates

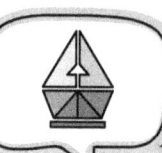
2. What did Abraham Lincoln propose for reconstruction?

    A. a plan that easily allowed Confederate states to rejoin the Union

    B. a plan that guaranteed civil rights for formerly enslaved people

    C. a plan that allowed the military to occupy the South

    D. a plan that stopped Confederates from holding political office

3. The Reconstruction Plan that succeeded was put through by ....

4. What was a reason why Republicans in Congress opposed Johnson's Reconstruction plan?

    A. They felt it would not unite the country fast enough.

    B. They felt it gave too many rights to African Americans.

    C. They felt it that it was not bipartisan enough.

    D. They felt it was too lenient on former Confederates.

Directions: Read the text and map below. Then answer the questions that follow.

"

During Reconstruction, the South was divided into five military districts. Armed forces occupied the South in order to enforce the Reconstruction laws. For the first few years of Reconstruction, freedmen and anti-slavery whites united, allowing the Republican Party to take political control of the South. However, over time, a backlash occurred, resulting in the Democratic Party taking political control of the region, state by state. The Democratic Party then established conservative governments that opposed Reconstruction. Reconstruction finally ended in 1877, when the Republican candidate for president, Rutherford B. Hayes, agreed to withdraw troops from the South in exchange for the presidency in a contested election.

"

1868 Date of readmission to the Union

1870 Date of reestablishment of conservative rule

Districts set up by Military Reconstruction Act, Mar. 2, 1867, and commanding generals

Gen. Schofield
Gen. Sickles
Gen. Pope
Gen. Ord
Gen. Sheridan

PA.
NJ.
OHIO
MD.
DEL.
ILL.
IND.
V.A.
Jan. 26, 1870
Oct. 5, 1869
W. VA.
KANSAS
MISSOURI
KENTUCKY
Military District No. 1
N.C.
Jun. 25, 1868
Nov. 3, 1870
TENN.
Jul. 24, 1866
Oct. 4, 1869
Military District No. 2
INDIAN
TERRITORY
ARK.
Jun. 22, 1868
Nov. 10, 1874
Military District No. 4
GA.
Jul. 15, 1870
Nov. 1, 1871
S.C.
Jun. 25, 1868
Nov. 28, 1876
NEW MEXICO
TERRITORY
ALA.
Jul. 14, 1868
Nov. 16, 1874
MISS.
Feb. 23, 1870
Jan. 4, 1876
Military District No. 3
ATLANTIC
OCEAN
TEXAS
Mar. 30, 1870
Jan. 14, 1873
Military District No. 5
L.A.
Jun. 25, 1868
Jan. 2, 1877
FLA.
Jun. 25, 1868
Jan. 2, 1877
MEXICO
GULF OF MEXICO

0   200   400 miles
0   200   400   600 kilometers

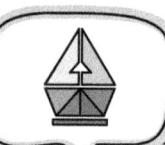
1. Which Southern state was not occupied by the military?

    A. Arkansas

    B. Tennessee

    C. Virginia

    D. Florida

2. What was the purpose of establishing military districts in the South after the Civil War?

    A. to enforce Reconstruction laws

    B. to defeat Confederate forces

    C. to allow the Democratic Party to stay in power

    D. to enforce the election of Rutherford B. Hayes

3. Which state was the last to reenter the Union?

    A. Texas

    B. Tennessee

    C. Florida

    D. Georgia

4. Which state was the first to be readmitted to the Union?

    A. Tennessee

    B. Florida

    C. South Carolina

    D. Texas

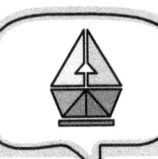
Directions: Read the text below. Then answer the questions that follow.

Reconstruction was a time of great change and violence in the South. Many southerners did not want African Americans to be equal to whites. Many viewed Reconstruction laws as being forced upon the South by the North. White northerners who moved to the South were mockingly called **carpetbaggers,** and white southerners who supported Reconstruction were called **scalawags**.

At first, under Andrew Johnson's plan, whites were allowed to set up their own governments. They immediately set up laws called the **Black Codes** that restricted the freedmen. When the federal government sent the military to occupy the South, the Black Codes ended, so many whites turned to violence through groups like the Ku Klux Klan. This group terrorized and often murdered African Americans and those that supported them. As Reconstruction ended and federal troops withdrew, southern state governments, led by politicians called Redeemers, passed laws that restricted African Americans' rights and segregated, or separated, them from white society. African Americans may have no longer been enslaved, but they still struggled with few rights in what became known as the **Jim Crow** era.

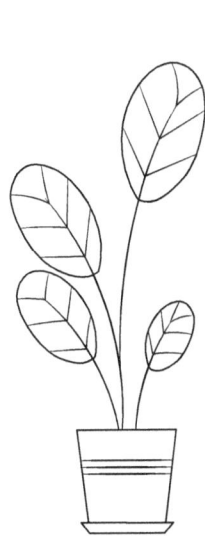

A political cartoon by Thomas Nast

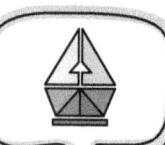
1. What was the purpose of the "Black Codes"? to restrict African American freedoms

    A. to use violence against African Americans

    B. to end the military occupation of the South

    C. to integrate African Americans into white society

2. What do you think was the purpose behind the political cartoon in this section?

....

....

3. Who were the scalawags?

    A. former enslaved African Americans

    B. northerners who moved to the South during Reconstruction

    C. southerners who supported Reconstruction

    D. southerners who led opposition to Reconstruction

4. Why do you think Redeemers called themselves by that name?

....

....

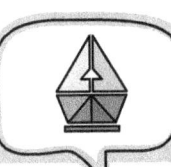
Directions: Read the text below. Then complete the exercise that follows.

Reconstruction had a tremendous impact on American history. Consider what issues today are linked to the issues of Reconstruction. Then draw a political cartoon or write a short poem to demonstrate this connection.

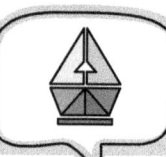
Directions: Read the text below. Then answer the questions that follow.

This week you learned about Reconstruction and its successes and failures. Consider Reconstruction and its impact while responding to the following questions.

1. Fill out the following chart identifying failures and successes of Reconstruction.

Successes	Failures

2. Would you consider Reconstruction a success or failure as a whole? Why or why not?

....

....

....

....

3. Looking back at Reconstruction, how do you think the federal government could have handled Reconstruction differently?

....

....

....

....

....

WEEK 2

Economics

Industrialization and Unionization

This week, you will learn about how industrialization advanced in the 19th and early 20th century and how changes to the economy resulted in action by workers.

ARGOPREP

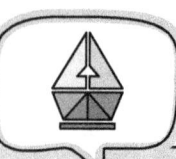
Directions: Read the text below. Then answer the questions that follow.

In the eighteenth and nineteenth centuries, there were advances in technology which led to massive **industrialization** in the United States. Industrialization meant that the country transformed from a reliance on agriculture to a reliance on the manufacturing of goods in factories. Inventions such as the spinning jenny, the steam engine, and sewing machines made the production of goods faster. **Interchangeable parts** in machines made machines easier to manufacture and maintain. Factories were established in cities, which began to attract people from rural areas. Transportation improvements, such as the Erie Canal in 1815, linked interior regions with large coastal cities. With the invention of the telegraph in 1844, people were able to send messages to one another almost instantly. The country was growing.

By the middle of the nineteenth century, this process sped up. Much of this was due to the invention of a cheaper way to make steel in 1856 by **Henry Bessemer**. More steel led to a great expansion of the country's railroad system, which resulted in a transportation revolution and allowed goods from the rural interior to be quickly shipped to coastal ports. Other innovations, such as the invention of the telephone by **Alexander Graham Bell** in 1867, greatly advanced communication.

Cities grew taller as cheaper steel and safer elevators allowed for the construction of the first skyscrapers. Of all the cities in the United States, New York grew the largest.

Much of the newly-created wealth came into the hands of a few people who created **monopolies**, called **trusts**. A monopoly is when a single business controls an entire industry. **Andrew Carnegie** became rich through his control of the steel industry. **John D. Rockefeller's** Standard Oil Company held a monopoly over the oil industry. **J.P. Morgan** was a powerful financier who was so rich he was able to help the federal government during two different economic crises. **Cornelius Vanderbilt** made his fortune in railroads.

Each of these powerful men accumulated a fortune that when adjusted for inflation made them far more wealthy than even the richest people today. They used their wealth to dominate their industries and prevent government reform. They also used their riches to help society. Carnegie, for example, funded the construction of almost 1,800 libraries in the United States. Rockefeller was a major philanthropist who donated his money to build colleges and universities.

People who disagreed with their ruthless business tactics accused them of being "robber barons." Those who believed that these men helped industrialize and advance the country called them "captains of industry."

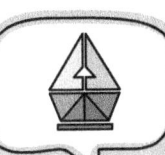
1. What is a monopoly?

   A. a single business that controls an industry
   B. the new inventions in technology that allowed denser cities to be built
   C. the innovations in agriculture that required more workers
   D. the improvements in transportation that allowed more immigrants to leave their countries

2. Why was Henry Bessemer's invention important?

   A. It revolutionized communication.
   B. It allowed machines to be made with interchangeable parts.
   C. It allowed the railroads to grow quickly and cities to build upward.
   D. It opened up a water route to the country's interior.

3. Which person made his fortune in the steel industry?

   A. J.P. Morgan
   B. Andrew Carnegie
   C. Cornelius Vanderbilt
   D. John D. Rockefeller

4. The foundation of an industrial economy is one based on ....

   A. manufactured goods
   B. agricultural products
   C. cheap steel
   D. advanced transportation

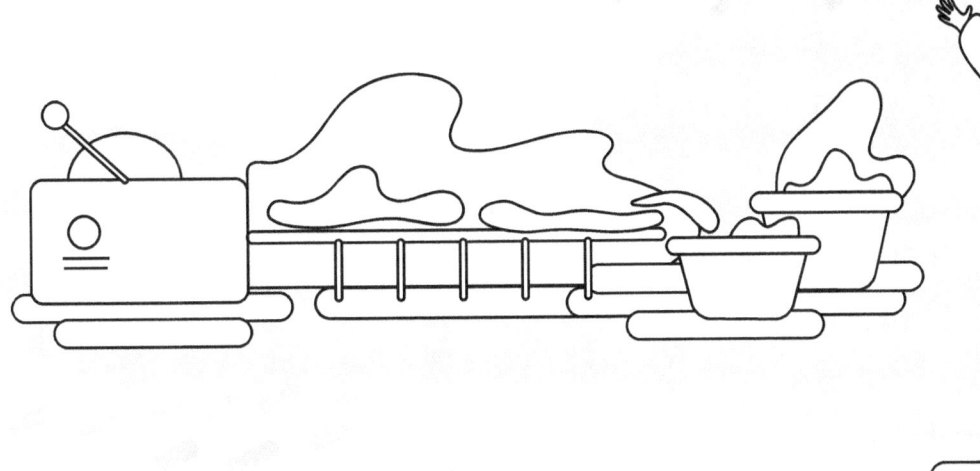

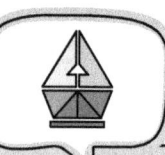
Directions: Read the text below. Then answer the questions that follow.

"

The wealthiest businessmen of the late 19th and early 20th century developed their fortunes through monopolies. Andrew Carnegie and John D. Rockefeller did this in different ways.

Andrew Carnegie was a poor Scottish immigrant who moved to the United States in 1848 at age 12. Andrew Carnegie used **vertical integration** to dominate the steel industry. Vertical integration is when a single company controls all the associated industries related to a particular industry. In Carnegie's case, this meant that he controlled not only the mills that made his steel but the iron mines from where the ore was taken, as well as the businesses that transported the steel. This allowed Carnegie to reduce costs, making his steel cheaper than the competition's.

Carnegie sold his steel company to J.P. Morgan in 1901 for $480 million, which equates to billions of dollars today. In his later years, Carnegie argued that the rich needed to give back to society, declaring, "The man who dies thus rich dies disgraced." He spent the rest of his life giving away his vast fortune before he died in 1919.

John D. Rockefeller was born in 1839 in upstate New York and concentrated his efforts on the oil refining industry. He founded the Standard Oil Company in 1870. Rockefeller used the same vertical integration tactics as Carnegie but he also used **horizontal integration**. Horizontal integration is when a company buys out other companies in the same industry. In Rockefeller's case, he drove down costs by offering cheaper products to the point where competitors could hardly stay in business. He then bought out the struggling competition. Rockefeller once said, "the growth of a large business is merely a survival of the fittest." By 1879, his Standard Oil Company controlled about 95% of oil refineries in the United States. Rockefeller spent the last forty years of his life as a philanthropist.

"

1. Which of the following would be an example of vertical integration?

   A. a lemonade stand controlling other lemonade stands

   B. a lemonade stand buying up lemon farms

   C. a lemonade stand controlling ice cream shops

   D. a lemonade stand working with other stands to control prices

2. What did Andrew Carnegie and John D. Rockefeller have in common?

    A. They were both immigrants.

    B. They were both philanthropists.

    C. They were both in the oil industry.

    D. They were both born wealthy.

3. What industry was John D. Rockefeller active in?

    A. finance

    B. railroads

    C. steel

    D. oil

4. How might Rockefeller and Carnegie's business methods impact the economy?

....

....

....

....

....

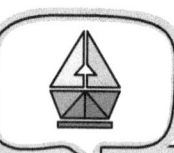
Directions: Read the text below. Then answer the questions that follow.

In the late 19th and early 20th centuries, people working for factories had few legal protections. Wages were low, hours were long, and conditions were dangerous. In 1912, up to 21,000 workers were killed in workplace accidents. The most notorious incident of the era was a fire at the **Triangle Shirtwaist Factory** in New York City on March 25, 1911. The building had one fire escape. When management locked its doors with workers still inside, 146 workers died. Most were young women.

To fight for themselves, workers organized unions. The first major unions were the **Knights of Labor, the American Federation of Labor**, and the **Industrial Workers of the World.**

* The Knights of Labor - Organized in 1869, it was the first large labor organization in the United States. It declined in importance in the 1890s.

* American Federation of Labor - Organized in 1886 and headed by Samuel Gompers, it represented mostly skilled workers.

* The Industrial Workers of the World - Founded in 1905, this labor union was international and represented skilled and unskilled workers. It was known for having more socialist positions than other labor organizations. They were nicknamed the "Wobblies."

One of the tools workers would use to fight for better pay and working conditions was the **strike**, or an organized work stoppage. Some of the most notable early strikes included:

* **Homestead Strike** - In 1892, workers striking the Carnegie Steel Company resulted in 16 deaths when private guards clashed with workers. The governor of Pennsylvania broke the strike with state troops.

* **Pullman Strike** - In 1894, railroad workers staged a large scale strike to which President Grover Cleveland intervened on behalf of the railroad companies.

* **The International Ladies Garment Workers Strike** - In 1909, mainly young women went on strike in the garment industry in New York. They successfully won better pay and shorter hours.

1. Who did the American Federation of Labor represent?

   A. steel workers

   B. garment workers

   C. skilled workers

   D. agricultural workers

2. What was the Triangle Shirtwaist Factory most known for?

   A. dangerous working conditions

   B. low pay

   C. child labor

   D. labor strikes

3. What might be the perspective taken by a business person representing the Carnegie Steel Company during the Homestead Strike?

   ....

   ....

   ....

4. How might Grover Cleveland have justified intervening during the Pullman Strike?

   ....

   ....

   ....

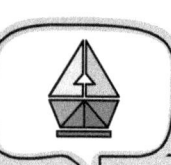
Directions: Read the text below. Then answer the questions that follow.

> Mark Twain wrote a novel titled *The Gilded Age* which was set during the time he lived in the late 1800s. Gilded means to coat something thinly with gold paint or leaf. Some scholars have called our own time period a Second Gilded Age.

1. What do you think Mark Twain meant by calling the time he lived in the "Gilded Age"?

2. How does the cartoon in this section demonstrate the problems of the Gilded Age?

3. What might be some similarities between Mark Twain's "Gilded Age" and our own time?

....

....

....

....

4. What might be some differences between Mark Twain's "Gilded Age" and our own time?

....

....

....

....

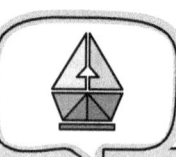
Directions: Read the text below. Then answer the questions that follow.

This week you learned about the development of industry and unions in the late 19th century. Consider these developments as you respond to the following questions.

1. What were the benefits of the Gilded Age to the United States?

....

....

....

2. Based on the problems of workers in the late 19th century, what do you think was the best way to solve their problems?

....

....

....

3. Is the cartoon to the right sympathetic to Andrew Carnegie? Why or why not?

....

....

....

....

....

....

....

....

....

....

4. Do you believe that Carnegie and Rockefeller's philanthropy outweighed their questionable practices? Explain.

_____

_____

_____

_____

_____

_____

WEEK 3

History
Immigration

This week, you will learn about the vast increase in immigration to the United States in the late 1800s and early 1900s and how the country reacted to it.

ARGOPREP

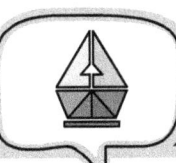
Directions: Read the text below. Then answer the questions that follow.

After the Civil War, industrialization generated economic growth within the United States. Factories in cities created jobs which drew people to migrate to the cities, especially from rural areas. Cities grew taller as cheaper steel and **safer elevators** allowed for the construction of the first **skyscrapers**. This allowed cities to grow denser with tall buildings. Of all the cities in the United States, New York grew the largest.

In 1800, the population of what would become the City of Greater New York was approximately 79,000 people. By 1850, this number had risen to 696,000, and in 1900 New York's population was well over 3 million.

Much of the growth of the cities was due to **immigration**. Immigrants were attracted to the United States for its wealth, freedom, and promise of work. In 1850, almost ten percent of the country's population was foreign-born. By 1910, this share had grown to almost 15 percent. Between 1880 and 1920, over two million immigrants moved into the United States, looking for a new start.

The journey of immigrants was challenging. Most immigrants during this time were processed through **Ellis Island** in New York Harbor if coming from Europe or **Angel Island** in San Francisco Bay if coming from Asia. In total, Ellis Island processed some 12 million immigrants. The vast majority of immigrants traveled by steamship, usually in the lower decks where poorer people could afford the fare.

At Ellis Island, immigrants were given a physical exam and completed a questionnaire that asked 29 questions regarding their race, why they were coming to America, and whether they had a trade. Usually this process took only a few minutes.

Those who passed the exam entered the United States where they would look for work and face new challenges and hardships.

1. How did industrialization help draw immigrants to the United States?

   A. The development of jobs in factories attracted people to move to the country.

   B. The new inventions in technology allowed denser cities to be built.

   C. The innovations in agriculture required more workers.

   D. The improvements in transportation allowed more immigrants to leave their countries.

2. Why was cheap steel important?

    A. It revolutionized communication.

    B. It allowed machines to be made with interchangeable parts.

    C. It allowed cities to become denser.

    D. It opened up a water route to the country's interior.

3. What was the main purpose of Angel Island?

    A. to process immigrants on the west coast

    B. to help immigrants obtain jobs

    C. to detain immigrants

    D. to find homes for immigrants

4. How did most immigrants travel to the United States?

    A. by railroad

    B. by steamship

    C. by airplane

    D. by foot

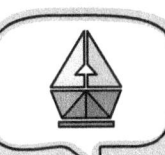
Directions: Read the text below. Then answer the questions that follow.

"

Many different groups of immigrants came to the United States in the 19th and early 20th centuries. They came in waves. The first major wave brought with it people from Ireland. Many came as a result of a fungus which destroyed much of Ireland's potato crop starting in 1845. The resulting famine drove millions of Irish to immigrate to the United States. At the same time, many Germans also moved to the United States seeking better work and escaping disruptive political conditions. In the 1850s, Chinese immigrants arrived looking for jobs; they contributed greatly to the construction of the country's railroads.

A second wave of immigration came in the 1880s. Many of these immigrants came from eastern, southern, and central Europe. This included more than four million Italians seeking good paying jobs and over two million Jews from central and eastern Europe escaping religious persecution.

Immigration to the United States 1850-1920

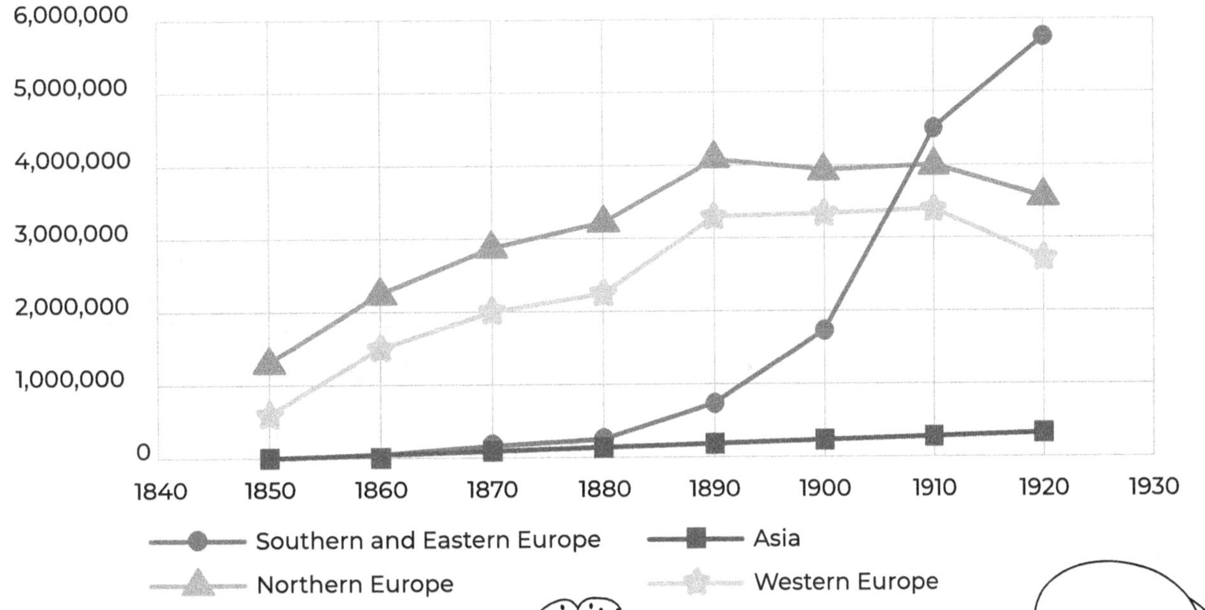

Southern and Eastern Europe ● Asia ■
Northern Europe ▲ Western Europe ★

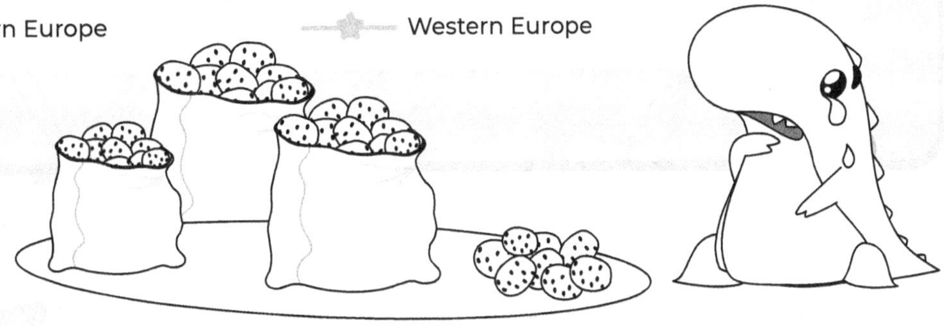

35
"

"

Many of the immigrants who came to the United States often faced harsh conditions. They were generally discriminated against and obtained low paying jobs under often dangerous conditions. Child labor was common. Most immigrants lived in the growing cities in apartments called **tenements**. These crowded buildings were poorly lit, not well ventilated, and subject to frequent fires. The conditions faced by immigrants would eventually lead to calls for reform.

"

1. What was a main reason why many Irish immigrated to the United States in the 19th Century?

   A. to have better paying jobs

   B. to get relief from political oppression

   C. to have religious freedom

   D. to escape famine and starvation

2. According to the graph in this section, in what year did immigrants from southern and eastern Europe overtake immigrants from other regions?

   ....

3. Which group of immigrants is known for having helped construct the country's railroads?

   A. Irish   **C.** Chinese

   B. German   **D.** Italian

4. What was a tenement?

   A. a crowded apartment building in a city

   B. a low-paying job at a factory

   C. a document that allowed immigrants to enter the country

   D. a method of child labor

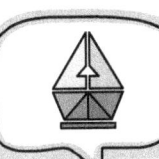
Directions: Read the text below. Then answer the questions that follow.

> Increased immigration to the United States caused a reaction among many of those who were native-born Americans. They resented immigrants entering America with different customs and religions. They argued that foreigners were taking jobs away from them. As a result, there was a growth of **nativism,** or the belief that native-born citizens should be treated better than immigrants. Nativists eventually succeeded in passing anti-immigration legislation.
>
> * 1882 - The Chinese Exclusion Act prevented the immigration of Chinese laborers.
>
> * 1907 - The Gentleman's Agreement was an informal agreement between the United States and Japan which stopped the immigration of Japanese into the United States.
>
> * 1917 - The United States established literacy tests which limited the number of immigrants entering the country.
>
> * 1924 - The Immigration Act of 1924 limited the number of immigrants into the United States using a quota system. It excluded Asians from immigrating to the United States except Japanese and Filipinos.

A political cartoon depicting a bias toward immigrants from Europe

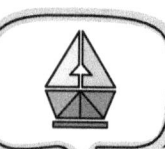
" These laws were not fully lifted until the 1960s. However, not all people were nativist. Some went into the tenements to photodocument immigrant life, such as Jacob Riis in his book, *How the Other Half Lives* (1890). People were beginning to understand the conditions immigrants were struggling under. "

1. Why do you think the anti-immigration laws of the 19th and 20th century targeted Asian groups more than other nationalities?

....

....

....

....

....

2. How do you think Jacob Riis meant to impact his readers through photographs?

....

The inside of a New York City tenement, photo by Jacob Riis

....

....

3. How did cultural bias or prejudice impact immigration policies?

A. Immigration was restricted to those who were educated.

B. Immigration laws favored those from Europe.

C. Immigration was limited from all countries.

D. Immigration laws encouraged diversity.

4. What was an economic argument used by nativists against immigration?

A. that immigrants were taking jobs away from native-born citizens

B. that immigrants were causing unsafe working conditions

C. that immigrants were overpopulating the country

D. that immigrants were destroying native businesses

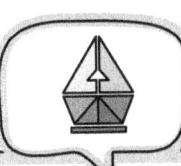
Directions: Read the text below. Then respond to the exercise that follows.

Immigrants to America had to undergo many hardships and had different reasons for leaving their home countries. In this exercise, take on the role of an immigrant in the 19th century. Write a letter to your home country describing what you are doing, your hopes, and your worries. You should include your country of origin, the reasons why you immigrated to the United States, and what troubles you have encountered.

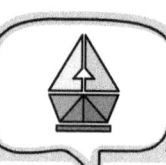
Directions: Read the text below. Then answer the questions that follow.

This week you learned about immigration to the United States during the 19th and early 20th centuries. Consider what you have learned when responding to the following questions.

1. How can the immigration experience from the past be similar to the immigrant experience today?

....

....

....

....

2. How do you think immigrants contributed to the United States?

....

....

....

....

3. Sometimes, America has been described as a "melting pot" due to the many immigrants who have come here. Do you think the term "melting pot" is accurate? What might be another term?

....

....

....

....

....

....

....

4. A poem by Emma Lazarus at the base of the Statue of Liberty reads in part:

Give me your tired, your poor,

Your huddled masses yearning to breathe free,

The wretched refuse of your teeming shore.

Send these, the homeless, tempest-tost to me,

I lift my lamp beside the golden door!

Based on the poem, how does Lazarus match fundamental concepts of American society to immigration?

....

....

....

....

WEEK 4

Civics and Government

The Progressive Era

This week, you will learn about the Progressives, reformers who tried to address problems in American society caused by industrialization.

ARGOPREP

Directions: Read the text below. Then answer the questions that follow.

"

The United States in the late 19th century had many problems that people began to recognize and attempted to reform. These people were known as the **Progressives**, and they wanted to build a better society. They were often inspired by religion. The time period where Progressives had the most influence on reform in the United States is referred to as the **Progressive Era**.

Progressives were interested in changing many aspects of society. Some wanted to regulate child labor. Many wanted to outlaw the sale of alcohol. Others wanted to eliminate corruption in government and make it more democratic. Others wanted to end monopolies.

Some Progressives spread information about problems through photographs, as did photographer Jacob Riis, whom you learned about last week. Riis published photographs documenting the harsh lives of immigrants. Others wrote articles or books. **Ida Tarbell** wrote a book in 1904 documenting the ruthless business practices of John D. Rockefeller's Standard Oil Company. People like Tarbell and Riis were called **muckrakers**. These were people who wanted to expose corruption.

Others attempted to reform society through charity or political action. **Jane Addams** became a notable Progressive reformer by helping to found Hull House in Chicago. **Hull House** was a settlement house in which educated women shared knowledge with and offered services to the poor. **Booker T. Washington** was a former slave who fought against the lynching of African Americans. **W.E.B. Dubois** was an African American who helped to found the **National Association for the Advancement of Colored People** (NAACP) in order to fight for African American rights. One of the most powerful Progressive leaders was **Theodore Roosevelt**, who was president of the United States from 1900 to 1908.

The efforts of the Progressives would lead to important reforms in American society. Congress passed the **Clayton Antitrust Act** in 1890 and the **Sherman Antitrust Act** in 1914 which banned monopolies and unfair business practices. The 17th Amendment ratified in 1913 allowed for the direct election of Senators. The 18th Amendment banned the sale and manufacture of alcohol in the United States. The 19th Amendment gave women the right to vote.

In addition to these amendments, laws were passed at the state and local levels that regulated working conditions and instituted safe practices. States also adopted legislative reforms such as referendum, initiative, and recall, which allowed voters to have a direct say in the creation of laws. The conservation movements also began during this era with the establishment of the first national parks.

"

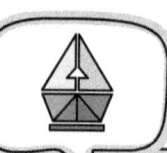
1. Which of the following Progressives established Hull House in Chicago?

   A. Ida Tarbell

   B. Jane Addams

   C. Jacob Riis

   D. Booker T. Washington

2. What did Ida Tarbell write about?

   A. the lynching of African Americans

   B. child labor

   C. the life of immigrants in the cities

   D. the business practices of Standard Oil

3. What did the 17th Amendment do?

   A. It allowed for the direct election of senators.

   B. It prohibited the sale of alcohol.

   C. It gave women the right to vote.

   D. It prohibited monopolies

4. Who was one of the founders of the National Association for the Advancement of Colored People?

   A. Ida Tarbell

   B. W.E.B. Dubois

   C. Booker T. Washington

   D. Jane Addams

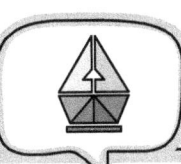

Directions: Read the text below. Then answer the questions that follow.

The following passage is an excerpt from Upton Sinclair's novel, *The Jungle* (1906) which describes a meatpacking plant in Chicago:

There would be meat that had tumbled out on the floor, in the dirt and sawdust, where the workers had tramped and spit uncounted billions of consumption germs. There would be meat stored in great piles in rooms; and the water from leaky roofs would drip over it, and thousands of rats would race about on it. It was too dark in these storage places to see well, but a man could run his hand over these piles of meat and sweep off handfuls of the dried dung of rats. These rats were nuisances, and the packers would put poisoned bread out for them; they would die, and then rats, bread, and meat would go into the hoppers together. This is no fairy story and no joke; the meat would be shoveled into carts, and the man who did the shoveling would not trouble to lift out a rat even when he saw one-- there were things that went into the sausage in comparison with which a poisoned rat was a tidbit. There was no place for the men to wash their hands before they ate their dinner, and so they made a practice of washing them in the water that was to be ladled into the sausage.

As a result of Sinclair's novel, the federal government passed and President Theodore Roosevelt signed the Meat Inspection Act in 1906 which fought to ensure that consumers purchased clean meat. Roosevelt also signed the Pure Food and Drug Act that same day which added significant protections for consumers. Food and drugs now had to be labeled with their ingredients.

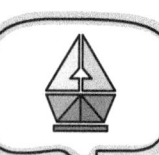
1. Based on the passage, Upton Sinclair was most likely a

   A. reformer
   B. politician
   C. muckraker
   D. business person

2. What do you think the purpose behind the author's passage was?

   ....

   ....

   ....

3. What was the impact of Sinclair's novel?

   ....

   ....

   ....

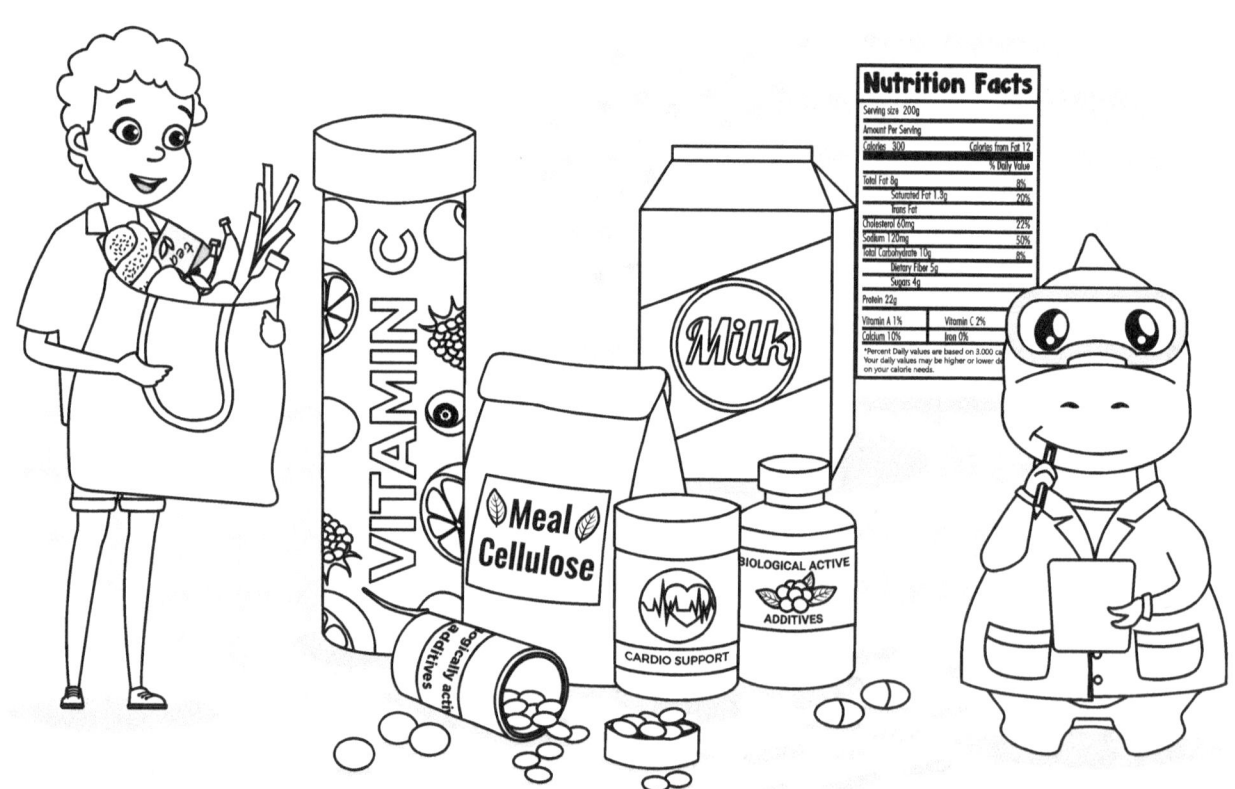

Directions: Read the text below. Then answer the questions that follow.

During the late 19th century, local and state governments were often in the hands of **political machines**. Political machines were party organizations that controlled enough votes to completely control a local government. These political machines were known for their corruption and gave out jobs to their supporters in return for votes and backing. The most notorious political machine was **Tammany Hall** in New York City.

One of the great achievements of the Progressive Era was making steps to reform local and state government. Some of these reforms included:

* **Initiative** - If enough citizens petition the government to change or add a law, it is then put out for a vote on referendum.

* **Referendum** - Citizens could vote directly on a law or issue on a ballot.

* **Recall** - If enough voters sign a petition, then a recall election can remove an elected official from office.

* **City Managers** and **commissioners** - Cities began appointing professional managers to administer cities and towns who were apolitical.

1. Explain some of the benefits of using initiative, referendum, and recall.

....

....

....

....

....

2. Explain what may be some of the downsides of an initiative, referendum, and recall.

....

....

....

....

....

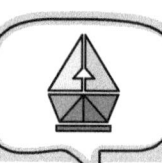
3. Explain how a city manager may help to reduce the influence of political machines.

....

....

....

4. Explain the difference between an initiative and referendum.

....

....

....

Directions: Read the text below. Then respond to the exercise that follows.

1. What would be an example of a muckraker today?

2. The Progressives worked to try to improve society and government in many areas. What might be a couple of areas of society and government that you think need reform today? How would you recommend doing it?

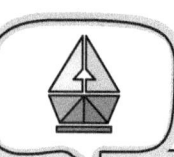
Directions: Read the text below. Then answer the questions that follow.

This week you learned about some of the aspects of the Progressive movement. Consider what you have learned when responding to the following questions.

1. Were the Progressives effective in bringing attention to problems of their day? Why or why not?

2. What areas of Progressive reform were most successful?

3. What areas of Progressive reform do you think were least successful? Why?

4. Elaborate on how the reforms of the Progressive Era have a direct impact on people today.

WEEK 5

History

Western Expansion After the Civil War

This week, you will learn how the United States settled the West after the Civil War and its conflicts with Native Americans.

ARGOPREP

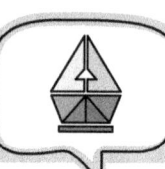
Directions: Read the text below. Then answer the questions that follow.

"

After the Civil War, the United States continued to expand westward. A major milestone of western settlement was the construction of a **transcontinental railroad** which was completed on May 10, 1869. The railroad allowed for faster access across the country. Instead of a 3,000 mile journey that was made in months by land or sea, the trek from the East Coast to the West Coast could be done in under a week. This allowed valuable resources from the west to be shipped east and connected the country. It sped up western settlement.

Washington Territory

Montana Territory

Oregon

Dakota Territory

Idaho Territory

Wyoming Territory

Minnesota

Wisconsin

Michigan

New Hampshire Maine

Vermont

New York

Massachusetts

Rhode Island

Connecticut

Nevada

Utah Territory

Nebraska

Iowa

Illinois

Indiana

Ohio

West Virginia

Pennsylvania

New Jersey

Delaware

Maryland

D.C.

California

Colorado

Kansas

Missouri

Kentucky

Virginia

(D.C. = District of Columbia)

North Carolina

Arizona Territory

New Mexico Territory

Neutral Strip

Indian Territory (Unorganized)

Arkansas

Tennessee

South Carolina

Greer Country (disputed between Texas and Indian Territory)

Mississippi

Alabama

Georgia

Texas

Louisiana

Florida

| States |
| Territories |
| Other countries |
| Disputed areas |

Kingdom of Hawaii

(not to scale)

District of Alaska

States and Territories of the United States of America
May 17, 1884 to November 2, 1889

"

"

Another important reason for western settlement was the **Homestead Act** which was signed into law by President Abraham Lincoln in 1862. The law allowed for people to claim free land in the west if they were willing to settle it. Prior to the Civil War, settlers generally crossed over the vast western states to the West Coast. Now, they moved to settle formerly ignored areas like the Great Plains. Technological innovations such as John Deere's **steel plow** made it possible to cut through the tough soil of the plains for agriculture.

American settlement came at a price for the Native Americans who lived in the West. As settlers moved into the region, they came into increasing conflict with the Native Americans who lived in the region. Native Americans were displaced by American settlers either through war or forced settlement onto reservations.

"

1. What new technology helped settlers farm in the West?

A. railroad

B. steel

C. canals

D. irrigation

2. What was a motive for people to settle in the west after the Civil War?

A. to escape political unrest

B. to mine for gold

C. to obtain free land

D. to look for jobs in cities

3. What was the impact of the transcontinental railroad on the American economy?

A. It allowed goods to be shipped to markets quickly.

B. It allowed people to migrate across the country quickly.

C. It allowed mail and messages to be delivered rapidly.

D. It allowed the military to be mobilized effectively.

4. According to the map in this section, which two states were once merged into a single territory?

A. Texas and Oklahoma

B. North and South Carolina

C. Idaho and Wyoming

D. North and South Dakota

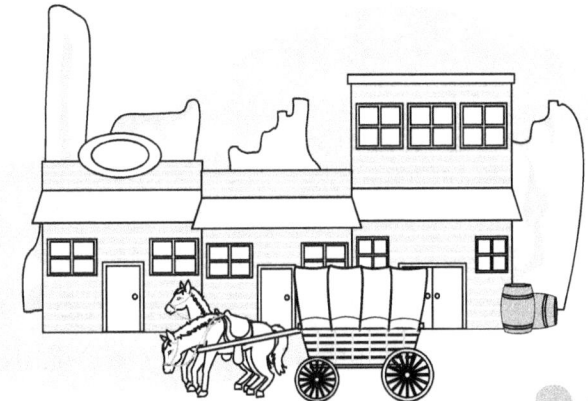

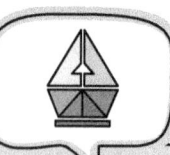
Directions: Read the text below. Then answer the questions that follow.

Native Americans came into conflict with white settlers as they pushed into their territories. Unfortunately, Americans and Native Americans had been in conflict since colonial days. In the years before the Civil War, Native Americans were pushed out of lands east of the Mississippi. Now with settlers pressing into the lands west of the Mississippi, conflict rose again.

The first major conflict was called **Red Cloud's War** in what is today Wyoming. From 1866 to 1868, Native Americans led by the Lakota chief Red Cloud attacked American settlers and soldiers in order to preserve their lands. This resulted in the **Treaty of Fort Laramie** which established a large reservation. It was a win for the Native Americans, but after gold was discovered in the Black Hills, the U.S. Army set up outposts in the region.

Tensions boiled over again at the **Battle of Little Bighorn**. At this battle, the American general **George Armstrong Custer**, was overwhelmed by Sioux and Cheyenne warriors led by the Sioux warrior **Crazy Horse**. Six hundred U.S. soldiers were killed by approximately 3,000 Native American warriors in what became known as Custer's Last Stand. Despite these victories, the U.S. Government was able to force the Sioux off their land.

Other wars and battles followed throughout the region. Americans slaughtered American bison during this time in part because it was a major resource for Native Americans on the Great Plains. The last major conflict was the **Wounded Knee Massacre** of 1890 where U.S. soldiers killed 146 Sioux "Ghost Dancers" who believed that the gods were angry with them for rejecting traditional Native American beliefs.

The American government also used laws to try to get Native Americans to abandon their traditional culture. **The Dawes Act** of 1887 declared that reservation land was to be broken up and allotted to individual Native Americans. This decision was supposed to to encourage Native Americans to take up farming. At the same time the act promised citizenship to Native Americans who adopted American customs and culture. Boarding schools were established where children were kept from the influence of their parents.

The policy of controlling Native Americans ended with the passage of the **Indian Reorganization Act** of 1934 which gave much power back to Native American tribes on their reservations.

1. What was the policy of the Dawes Act?

    A. to remove Native Americans east of the Mississippi

    B. to establish Native American reservations

    C. to Americanize Native Americans

    D. to push the U.S. Army into Native American territories

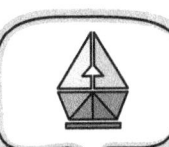

2. What occurred at Little Big Horn?

    A. a defeat for American soldiers

    B. a massacre of Native Americans

    C. the signing of a treaty

    D. the establishment of a reservation

3. What kind of assumptions do you think the people who passed the Dawes Act made?

....

....

....

4. What do you think was the primary reason why Americans took control of Native American territories?

....

....

....

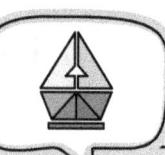
Directions: Read the text below. Then answer the questions that follow.

"

You have learned much about the Native American wars of the late 19th century. One conflict occurred in the Oregon Territory when the Nez Perce were ordered to move to a reservation in Idaho. Their leader, **Chief Joseph**, agreed. However, after some of his tribe killed white settlers, he attempted to flee to Canada and fought skirmishes with the U.S. Army. Finally he surrendered on October 5, 1877 and sent this message to the American general:

Tell General Howard I know his heart. What he told me before, I have it in my heart. I am tired of fighting. Our Chiefs are killed; Looking Glass is dead, Ta Hool Hool Shute is dead. The old men are all dead. It is the young men who say yes or no. He who led on the young men is dead. It is cold, and we have no blankets; the little children are freezing to death. My people, some of them, have run away to the hills, and have no blankets, no food. No one knows where they are - perhaps freezing to death. I want to have time to look for my children, and see how many of them I can find. Maybe I shall find them among the dead. Hear me, my Chiefs! I am tired; my heart is sick and sad. From where the sun now stands I will fight no more forever.

"

1. What does Chief Joseph's speech explain about the relationship between the United States and Native American Tribes?

....

....

2. Explain how Chief Joseph's speech reflects Native American views of themselves during this era of conflict.

....

....

"

Directions: Read the text below. Then complete the activity that follows.

For this activity, print or draw a map of New York state and then conduct research as to the location of Native American reservations. Mark those locations with their names on the map.

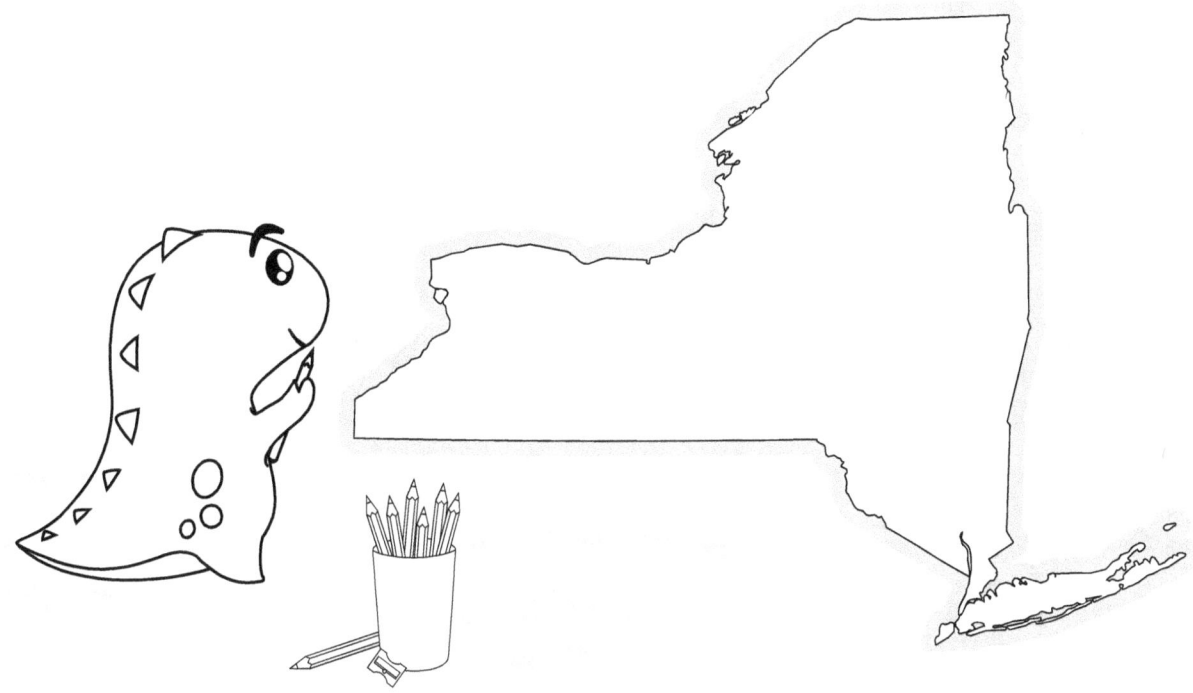

Directions: Read the text below. Then answer the questions that follow.

This week you learned about how technology spurred western settlement after the Civil War which resulted in the displacement of Native Americans. Consider that while responding to the following questions:

1. Summarize the policy of the U.S. government toward Native Americans.

....

....

....

....

2. Do you think conflict between the United States and Native Americans could have been avoided? Why or why not?

....

....

....

....

3. Elaborate on how advances in technology may lead to conflict using the United States' relationship with Native Americans as an example.

....

....

....

....

....

....

....

....

....

WEEK 6

Geography
American Imperialism

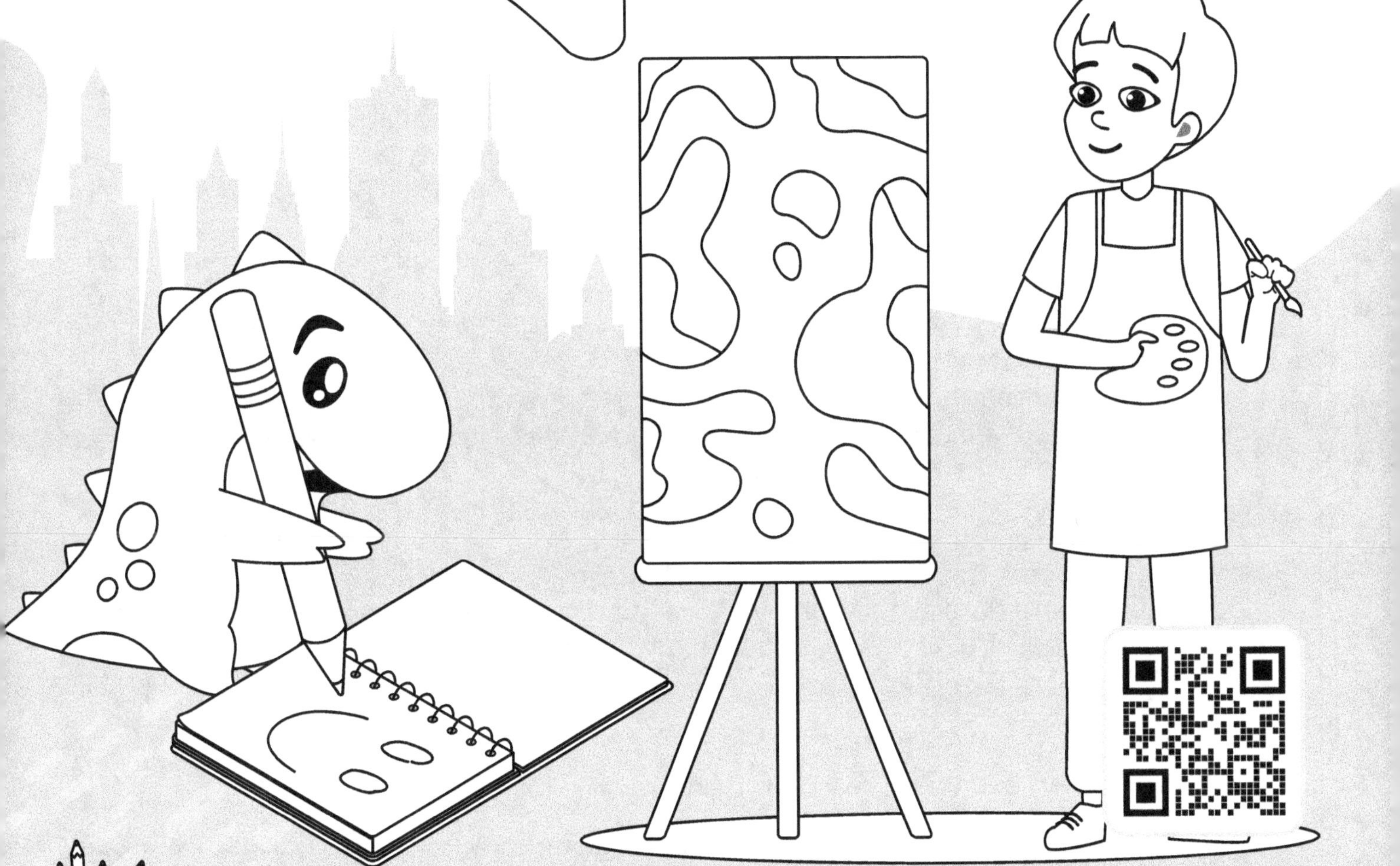

This week, you will learn about how the United States expanded its overseas territory and became an imperial power after the Spanish-American War.

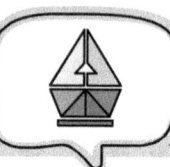
Directions: Read the text below. Then answer the questions that follow.

"

At the end of the 19th century, the United States expanded its power overseas. This happened at the same time that many European countries were also extending their power over other people and lands. This is called **imperialism**.

American imperialism was driven by economic, political, and social factors. Economically, the country was expanding and business leaders wanted to have new markets overseas to sell the many goods that were being produced by American industry. Politically, strategists believed imperialism was a good long-term strategy for the United States to have overseas bases to help protect American trade and expand American power. Also, there was a rivalry between powerful countries at this time to create overseas empires. Socially, there was a belief that those of European origin were superior to other races and that it was their duty to "civilize" foreign people. This included sending missionaries abroad to convert people to Christianity.

The step which made the United States an imperial country was the **Spanish-American War** of 1898. This war was caused by American objections to the harsh treatment of Cuban rebels by Spain. Tensions heightened when the battleship *Maine* exploded in Havana harbor after the ship was sent to protect American citizens and property in Cuba. The sinking is still a mystery. However, at the time, newspapers blamed it on the Spanish. Newspapers also published sensational accounts, called **yellow journalism**, of the suppression of the Cuban rebels which generated anti-Spanish sentiment. Tensions finally boiled over with declarations of war between Spain and the United States in April 1898.

The war resulted in an American victory. As a result, the United States acquired some of Spain's overseas empire. The United States gained the Philippines, Guam, and Puerto Rico. Cuba became its own nation, but it was dependent upon the United States. In addition, the United States annexed Hawaii during the war.

Theodore Roosevelt gained fame for organizing a regiment during the Spanish-American War known as the Rough Riders. He strongly supported American imperialism. Roosevelt became William McKinley's Vice President in 1900. The next year, McKinley was assassinated, and Roosevelt became president.

"

1. What was an economic reason for American expansion overseas?

    A. the motive to expand American naval power

    B. the desire to find new places to set up factories

    C. the belief that those of European origin were superior to others

    D. the desire for overseas markets to sell goods

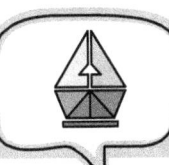
2. How did yellow journalism contribute to the Spanish-American War?

   A. It generated anti-Spanish opinion through sensational stories.

   B. It published accounts of how the United States needed to expand militarily.

   C. It provided accounts hostile to Cuban rebels.

   D. It published accounts of how the United States needed to annex Hawaii.

3. What was a social reason for American expansion overseas?

   A. a need for more overseas markets

   B. a belief that those of European origin were superior to other races

   C. a policy that the United States needed to expand its naval power

   D. a feeling of sympathy for oppressed Cubans

4. What was a cause of the Spanish-American War?

   A. the explosion of an American naval ship

   B. the harsh treatment of Spanish nationals by Cuba

   C. the desire for more markets to sell to overseas

   D. the acquisition of overseas territory by the United States

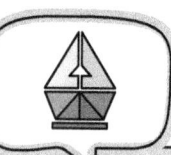

Directions: Read the text below. Then answer the questions that follow.

Yesterday, you learned about the causes of American overseas expansion which was triggered by the Spanish-American War. After the war, the United States acquired overseas territories and continued to expand its power and influence. This came at a price. In the Philippines, for example, many did not want to be controlled by the United States. This conflict resulted in a long war between Filipinos and the Americans between 1899 and 1902. About 200,000 people died from war, disease, and starvation during this time.

American ambitions intensified under President Theodore Roosevelt. In 1904, Roosevelt added onto the traditional foreign policy of the **Monroe Doctrine** in which President James Monroe asserted that European powers should not interfere in affairs in the Western Hemisphere. The **Roosevelt Corollary**, as it was called, reserved the right for the United States to intervene directly in the affairs of other countries in the Western Hemisphere.

To further expand American power, Roosevelt supported the building of the **Panama Canal**. The Panama Canal greatly reduced the travel time needed to travel by ship between the east and west coasts of the United States. In addition, the United States now had territories overseas and wanted to be able to send its navy to them quickly. At that time, Panama was controlled by Colombia. When Colombia rejected the terms of the proposed American canal, Roosevelt helped to support an independence movement in Panama. The new Panamanian government agreed to the American terms of $10 million dollars in a one time payment, as well as $250,000 annually. The United States controlled the canal zone, and the canal was completed in 1914.

These events marked the beginning of tense relations between the United States and Latin America.

San Francisco • • New York City

Atlantic Ocean

5,200 Miles
8,370 Kilometers

PANAMA CANAL

Equator

13,000 Miles
20,900 Kilometers

Pacific Ocean

1. What was a difference between the Monroe Doctrine and the Roosevelt Corollary?

   A. The Monroe Doctrine was more concerned with the affairs of Latin American countries than European ones.

   B. The Roosevelt Corollary expanded the United States' role in the affairs of other countries while the Monroe Doctrine did not.

   C. The Monroe Doctrine focused on using the American military while the Roosevelt Corollary focused on economic power.

   D. The Roosevelt Corollary declared neutrality in Latin American affairs while the Monroe Doctrine did not.

2. Describe how the United States intervened in the affairs of Colombia.

   ....

   ....

   ....

3. What was the main reason Theodore Roosevelt was interested in building a canal in Panama?

   A. A canal greatly increased the potential of trade with Latin America.

   B. A canal would allow the United States to establish colonies.

   C. A canal greatly increased the speed with which vessels could travel from the east to west coasts of the United States.

   D. A canal would lessen the influence of European countries in the Western Hemisphere.

4. What directly occurred because of the United States' acquisition of new territory in the Pacific?

   A. a rebellion in the Philippines

   B. an independence movement in Panama

   C. a project to build a canal across Latin America

   D. a new foreign policy expanding the Monroe Doctrine

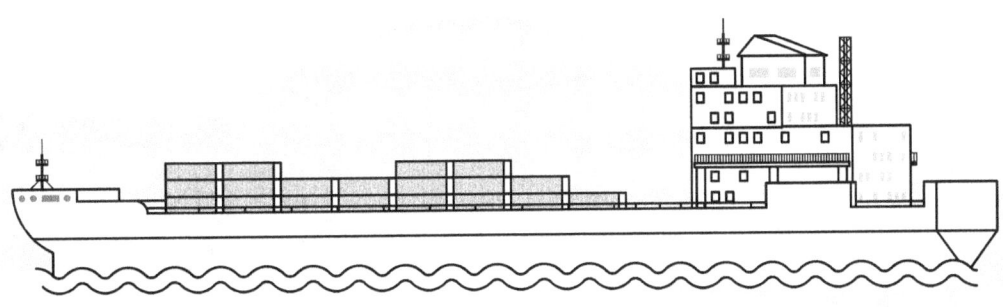

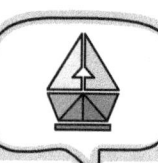
Directions: Read the text below. Then answer the questions that follow.

Political cartoons often express different points of view. The cartoons below depict Theodore Roosevelt and represent the conflicting views on American imperialism.

1. Which of the two political cartoons is more sympathetic toward Roosevelt?

2. What does the second cartoon say about Roosevelt's foreign policy?

3. How does the first cartoon contrast with the second cartoon?

....

....

....

....

4. How might these illustrations reflect public opinion about American overseas expansion?

....

....

....

....

Directions: Read the text below. Then answer the questions that follow.

American intervention overseas is a complex topic with divided opinions. Based on your reading and your knowledge of the state of the world today, consider the following questions.

1. When do you think it is justifiable for the United States to intervene in the affairs of other countries?

_____

_____

_____

_____

_____

2. How may the United States' relationship with Latin America today be partially explained by American expansion?

_____

_____

_____

_____

3. If you were living in a Latin American country during the era of American imperialism, what might be your viewpoint toward the United States?

_____

_____

_____

_____

_____

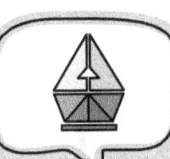
Directions: Read the text below. Then answer the questions that follow.

This week you learned about American imperialism and expansion overseas. Consider your readings when answering the following questions.

1. Do you think the United States would have been better served with a different foreign policy after the Spanish-American War? Why or why not?

....

....

....

2. Describe and elaborate on the impact of American overseas expansion.

....

....

....

3. What do you think was the most important cause of American imperialism? Elaborate on why you think that is the case.

....

....

....

4. What moral assumptions might Americans have been making to help justify overseas expansion? In your opinion, were these assumptions right or correct?

....

....

....

....

WEEK 7

History
World War I

This week, you will learn about World War I and how America came to be involved.

ARGOPREP

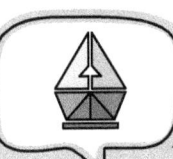

Directions: Read the text below. Then answer the questions that follow.

World War I began in 1914 after Franz Ferdinand, the archduke of Austria-Hungary, was assassinated. The murder triggered a series of events which resulted in the further pulling apart of two groups of countries. Germany, Austria-Hungary, the Ottoman Empire, and Bulgaria were called the **Central Powers**. France, Great Britain, Italy, Russia, and Japan were called the **Allies**. At the beginning of the war, the United States was neutral.

While the event that triggered the war was the assassination, there were deeper causes of World War I. The first was an alliance system that divided the most powerful countries in the world into two camps. Some of these alliances were secret and came into play after the archduke was killed. The second was imperialism; countries wanted to expand their power. The third was militarism; countries such as Great Britain and Germany had massive military build ups. The last reason was **nationalism**. Nationalism is the support of your own country over others. In extreme cases, nationalists believe that their own country is superior to others.

World War I was also called the Great War. Due to advances in technology, the war became a bloodbath, killing over 16 million people between 1914 and 1918. The United States tried not to get involved. President **Woodrow Wilson** ran for a second term of office in 1916 on the platform that he had kept the United States out of the war.

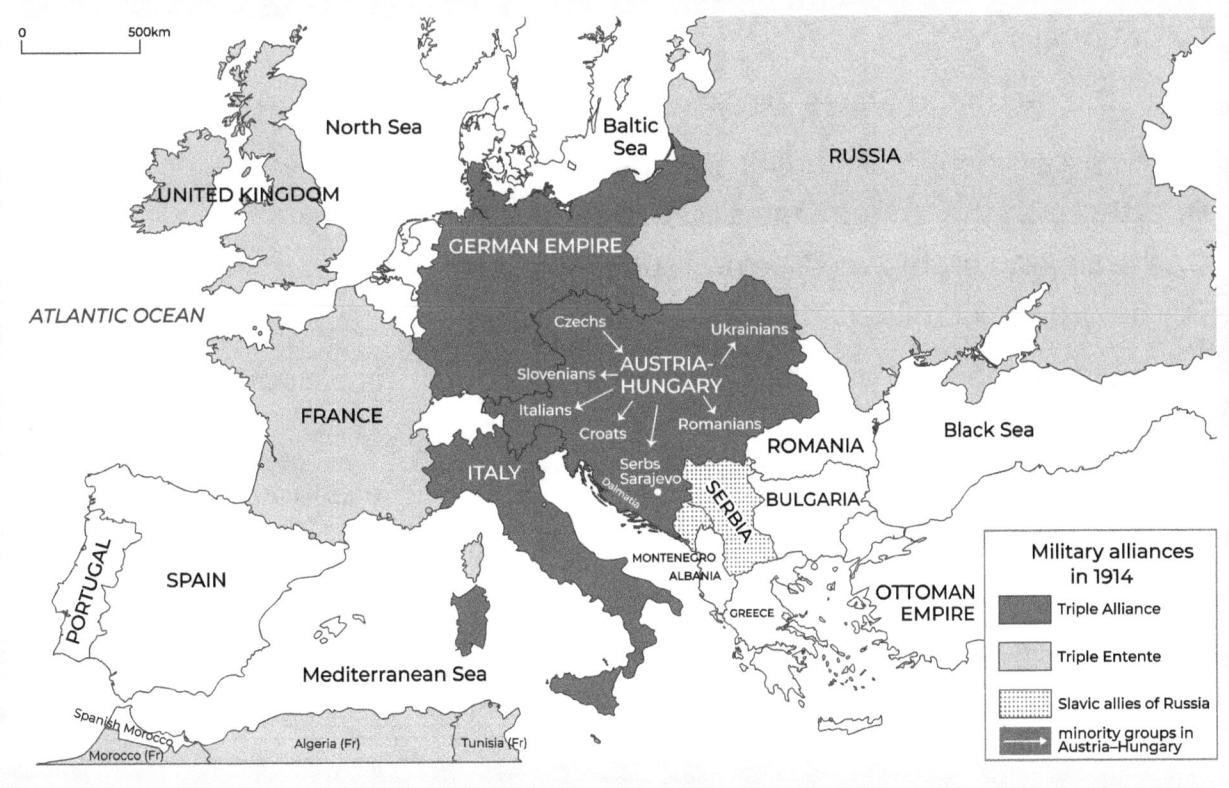

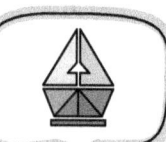
"
However, in 1917, the United States was drawn into the conflict on the side of the Allies. This was due to Germany's use of submarines to sink ships that were carrying war supplies to Europe. Some of those ships had American citizens aboard. The United States then sent soldiers to Europe. On November 11, 1918, the war ended with a victory for the Allies.
"

1. Which of the following was an immediate cause of World War I?

    A. the sinking of ships by German submarines

    B. the assassination of a political leader

    C. the development of alliance systems

    D. the growth of nationalism

2. What was a reason why World War I killed more people than other wars?

    A. advances in technology

    B. alliance systems

    C. political assassinations

    D. nationalism

3. Why did the United States join the fighting in World War I?

    A. the assassination of a political leader

    B. attacks on the United States by the Ottoman Empire

    C. the sinking of ships by German submarines

    D. the growth of militarism in the United States

4. The building of more guns and weapons in a country is part of what?

    A. militarism

    B. nationalism

    C. warfare

    D. industrialization

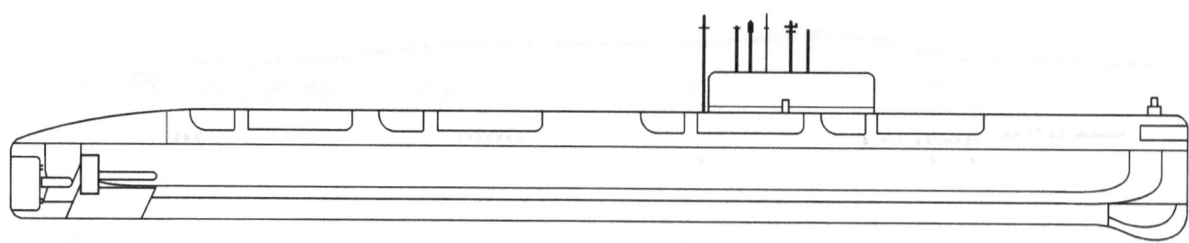

Directions: Read the text below. Then answer the questions that follow.

World War I was one of the bloodiest conflicts in human history. For example, at the **Battle of the Somme** between July and November in 1916, there were over one million casualties.

World War I was different from other wars before it because of its use of modern technology. Unfortunately, military leaders still used older forms of strategy that did not take into account the changes in technology, resulting in massive casualties. Perhaps one of the most important inventions used during the war was the machine gun. The machine gun was first invented in 1884 in the United States and was used extensively during World War 1. A machine gun pours out rapid rounds of ammunition which prevents enemy troops from advancing. In response, soldiers dug out long trenches and hid there for protection. The result was that two lines of trenches faced each other with little movement. The land between the trenches was destroyed by the fighting and called "no man's land." This type of fighting mostly occurred in France and is called **trench warfare.**

Another example of technology that was used for the first time in WWI was the airplane. At first, planes were used for scouting enemy positions from the skies. Later in the war, planes were armed with guns to directly attack the other side. On the ground, armies used the invention of the tank. These heavily armed machines withstood machine gun fire and could penetrate trenches. At sea, the Germans heavily used submarines, which they called U-boats, to attack enemy ships and shipping.

World War I also saw the use of chemical weapons such as poisonous gas. Germany first used gas in 1915 with terrible results. The Allies retaliated with chemical weapons as well. Chemical weapons were banned from use in war in 1925.

1. What advance in technology helped lead to trench warfare?

A. the airplane

B. the submarine

C. the tank

D. the machine gun

2. What type of weapon was banned after World War I?

A. chemical weapons

B. machine guns

C. submarines

D. tanks

3. How did changes in technology conflict with military strategy during World War I?

....

....

....

....

4. How does World War I demonstrate the downsides of advances in technology?

....

....

....

....

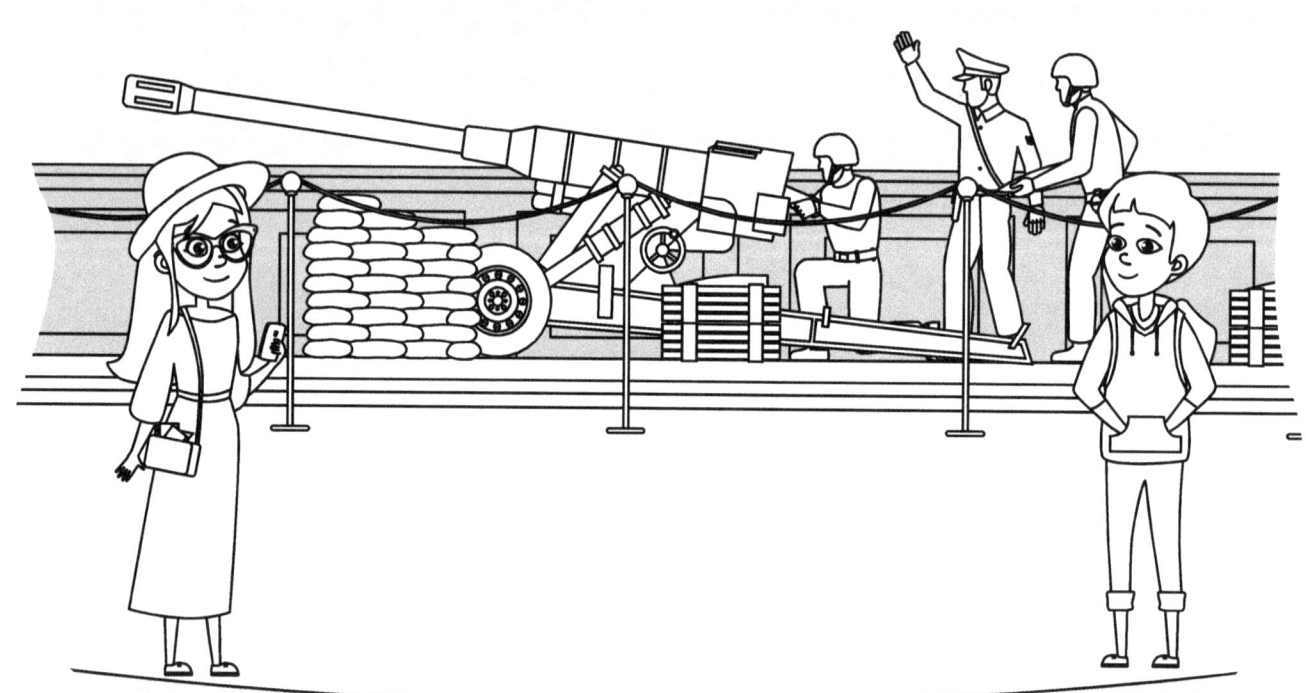

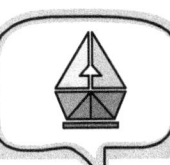
Directions: Read the text below. Then answer the questions that follow.

When World War I ended, President Woodrow Wilson called for the expansion of democracy. He presented a plan known as the **Fourteen Points** which he felt would create long-lasting peace. Some of the major initiatives Wilson proposed were as follows:

* No secret treaties or alliances

* Freedom of the seas where neutral countries could travel and trade to other countries without a threat of attack

* Arms reductions

* The creation of a League of Nations to settle international disputes

* Free trade between countries

* The right of **self-determination** for people of different nationalities to form their own countries

Some of Wilson's ideas were accepted and large empires were broken up into smaller countries. After the war, the **League of Nations** was founded and arms reduction treaties were signed. However, in the **Treaty of Versailles**- the treaty that ended the war- other Allied powers sought to punish Germany. They believed Germany to be the main aggressor and blamed the country for starting the war. They required Germany to make large payments, or reparations, to other Allied countries.

As for the United States, the Senate never ratified the Treaty of Versailles. Opposition leaders, such as **Henry Cabot Lodge** believed that the United States would give up too many of its rights by joining the League of Nations. Others thought that entering the League would draw the United States into more foreign conflicts. The United States eventually made a separate peace agreement with Germany.

1. Woodrow Wilson said he wanted a "peace without victory." Explain what Wilson meant by that statement.

....

....

....

....

....

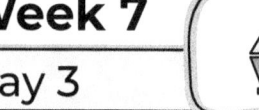

2. Explain why the United States might be especially interested in maintaining "freedom of the seas" in light of the events of World War I?

....

....

....

3. Explain the reasons why the Treaty of Versailles was rejected by the United States Senate.

....

....

....

4. Do you think that Woodrow Wilson's Fourteen Points were realistic? Explain your thinking.

....

....

....

Directions: Read the text below. Then answer the questions that follow.

Letters to and from home were important to soldiers fighting in the trenches. Through their letters, they shared their experiences not only with their families but with us today.

The following passage is an excerpt from a letter home by U.S. soldier Basil Beebe Elmer on August 5, 1918:

"... We were now near the front line ... We entered the line and drove, drove, drove. I can never describe it. It doesn't seem real. It is all a dream – a nightmare. Day after day, night after night, unceasingly. ... Ollie Ames and Joyce Kilmer are buried side by side at the edge of the wood ... I sat there yesterday, thinking. "Ollie, Ollie!" I thought of his wife and his mother. And I thought of you. How dear you two are to me! Nothing else matters to me – only you. ... what a wonderful thing [Ollie] has to pass on to his wife and daughter! I find myself thinking of Ollie constantly. I know I must stop, but he was my best friend and he died so bravely that I cannot forget."

1. How do letters home from soldiers provide good primary source material for historians?

....

....

....

....

2. How are experiences during historical events captured today? What is an advantage of using letters to capture experiences over other ways?

....

....

....

....

3. How can readers relate to the experiences of Elmer by reading his letter?

....

....

....

....

Directions: Read the text below. Then answer the questions that follow.

This week you learned about World War I, America's involvement in the war, and the peace treaty that followed.

1. What were problems with the Treaty of Versailles that could potentially lead to future conflict?

2. World War I was the first time the United States was heavily active in a major conflict overseas. What are the consequences of American military involvement overseas?

3. Do you believe that the causes of World War I could create a similar conflict today? Explain and elaborate.

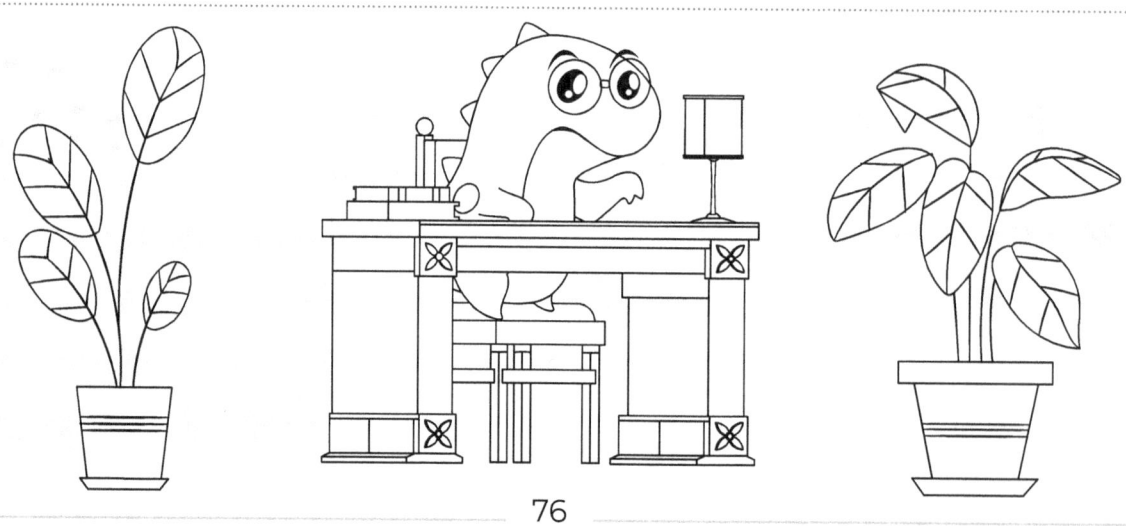

WEEK 8

History

Civil Rights After World War I

This week, you will learn about civil rights struggles after World War I, including the Women's Suffrage Movement and the fight for African American rights.

ARGOPREP

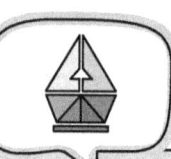
Directions: Read the text below. Then answer the questions that follow.

After World War I, there were changes to American politics that both expanded civil rights for women while at the same time laying the foundation for the expansion of civil rights for African Americans. In 1919, women won the right to vote through the ratification of the **19th Amendment**. This was the result of activism starting in 1848 when **Elizabeth Cady Stanton** and **Lucretia Mott** organized the **Seneca Falls Convention**, an event which began the push for women's rights. After the Civil War, Stanton and fellow activist **Susan B. Anthony** formed the **National Woman Suffrage Association** in 1869. This association pushed for a constitutional amendment to provide for women's **suffrage**, meaning the right to vote. Meanwhile, individual states started granting the right to vote through the efforts of the American Woman Suffrage Association which was founded by **Lucy Stone** and **Henry Blackwell**. In 1890, the two different suffrage organizations merged to form the National American Woman Suffrage Association which continued to push for women's voting rights at the state level. They were so successful that by the end of World War I, many individual states granted women the right to vote. Continued protests finally led to the adoption of the amendment, guaranteeing women's right to vote on a national level.

African Americans had been suffering under Jim Crow repression since Reconstruction. There was hope by some prominent African American activists, such as **W.E.B. Du Bois**, that participation in World War I would demonstrate that African Americans were as courageous and patriotic as white citizens.

African American veterans believed that their sacrifices and service had earned them equal rights. However, race riots and lynchings occurred frequently during the war. One major riot was the **East St. Louis Riot** in which dozens of African Americans were murdered. African Americans held a protest against the riots in New York by silently walking down Fifth Avenue. This was known as the **Silent March**.

Even after the war, racism and Jim Crow laws remained. In 1919, race riots erupted across the nation in what was called the Red Summer. Then in 1921, in what was possibly the most violent race riot in American history, an unknown number of African Americans were killed in the **Tulsa Race Riot**. While advances in civil rights were not forthcoming after the war, African Americans understood that they needed to organize to fight racism. This laid the seeds for the civil rights movement later in the century.

1. Who was a leader who advocated for African American rights?

    A. Henry Blackwell

    B. Elizabeth Cady Stanton

    C. W.E.B. Dubois

    D. Lucretia Mott

2. What did W.E.B. Dubois hope for?

    A. that African Americans would mobilize to protest racial injustices

    B. that states would grant women suffrage

    C. that African American's war service clearly demonstrated their right to equality

    D. that women would earn the right to vote peacefully

3. Where did the national movement for women's suffrage begin?

    A. East St. Louis

    B. New York

    C. Tulsa

    D. Seneca Falls

4. Which of the following was a protest against racial violence?

    A. the Silent March

    B. the East St. Louis Riot

    C. the Seneca Falls Convention

    D. the Tulsa Race Riot

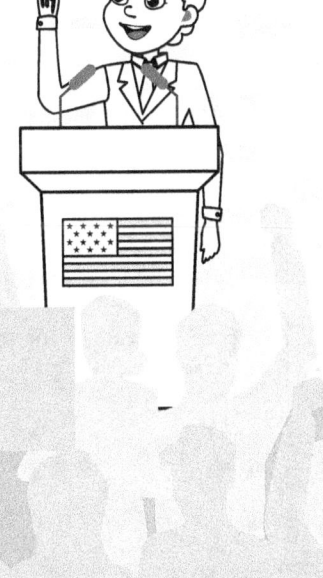

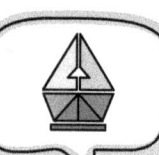
Directions: Read the text below. Then answer the questions that follow.

Women's suffrage occurred at a national level with the passage of the 19th Amendment in 1919. However, prior to 1919, many states offered some form of women's suffrage. Some states offered full suffrage which gave complete voting rights to women. Others only allowed women to vote in presidential elections. Some allowed voting in presidential and municipal elections. A few states granted women the right to vote only in school elections. In Florida, only certain charter cities gave women the right to vote at this time. Explore the map below, and then answer the questions that follow.

Women's Suffrage 1919

Map of the United States showing women's suffrage status by state:

- WA 1910
- OR 1912
- MT 1914
- ID 1896
- ND 1917
- MN 1919
- WI
- ME 1919
- VT
- NY 1917
- NH
- MA
- CT
- RI 1917
- MI 1918
- SD 1918
- WY 1869
- NE 1917
- IA 1919
- IL 1913
- IN 1919
- OH 1917
- PA
- NJ
- DE
- NV 1914
- UT 1896
- CO 1893
- KS 1912
- MO 1919
- KY
- WV
- VA
- CA 1911
- AZ 1912
- NM
- OK 1918
- AR 1917
- TN 1919
- NC
- SC
- TX 1918
- LA
- MS
- AL
- GA
- FL

Legend:
- Full Suffrage
- Presidential Suffrage
- Presidential & Municipal Suffrage
- Local School Elections
- Municipal Suffrage in Charter Cities
- No Suffrage

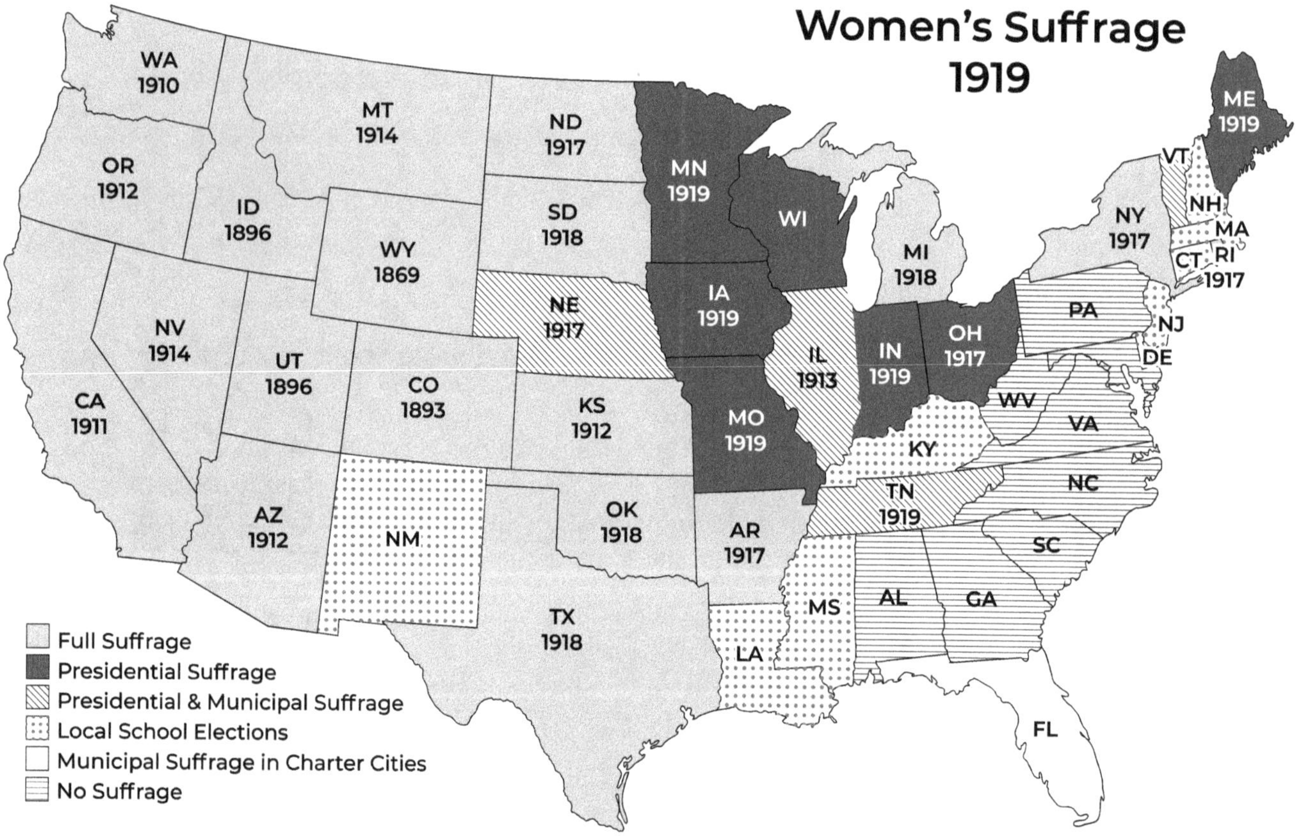

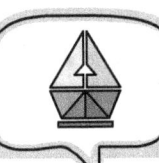
1. Which state was the earliest to offer full suffrage to women?

2. Which area of the country offered the most voting rights to women prior to 1919?

    A. the southeast

    B. the northeast

    C. the west

    D. the midwest

3. How many states only had limited suffrage before 1919?

    A. 22

    B. 8

    C. 4

    D. 18

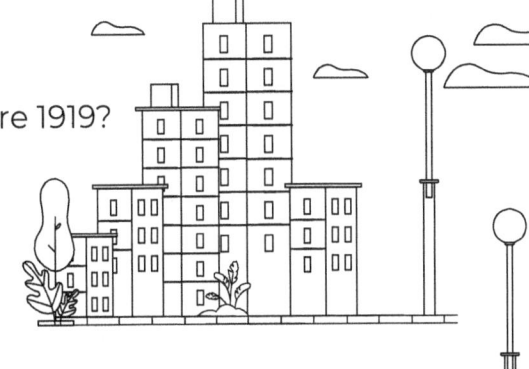

4. What does this map tell you about the process of women's suffrage?

    A. It shows no geographic pattern.

    B. It was inconsistent until the 19th Amendment was passed.

    C. It shows that women in the Northeast had more rights than women in the West.

    D. It shows that a minority of states had no suffrage rights before 1919.

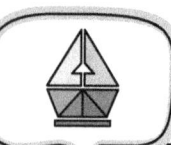
Directions: Read the text below. Then answer the questions that follow.

"

After the Civil War, more than 90% of African Americans in the United States lived in the South. This remained the case until the early 20th century. However, after World War I, African Americans from primarily rural areas began moving to more urban areas in the north and midwest.This movement of people has been called the **Great Migration** by historians and lasted until 1970.

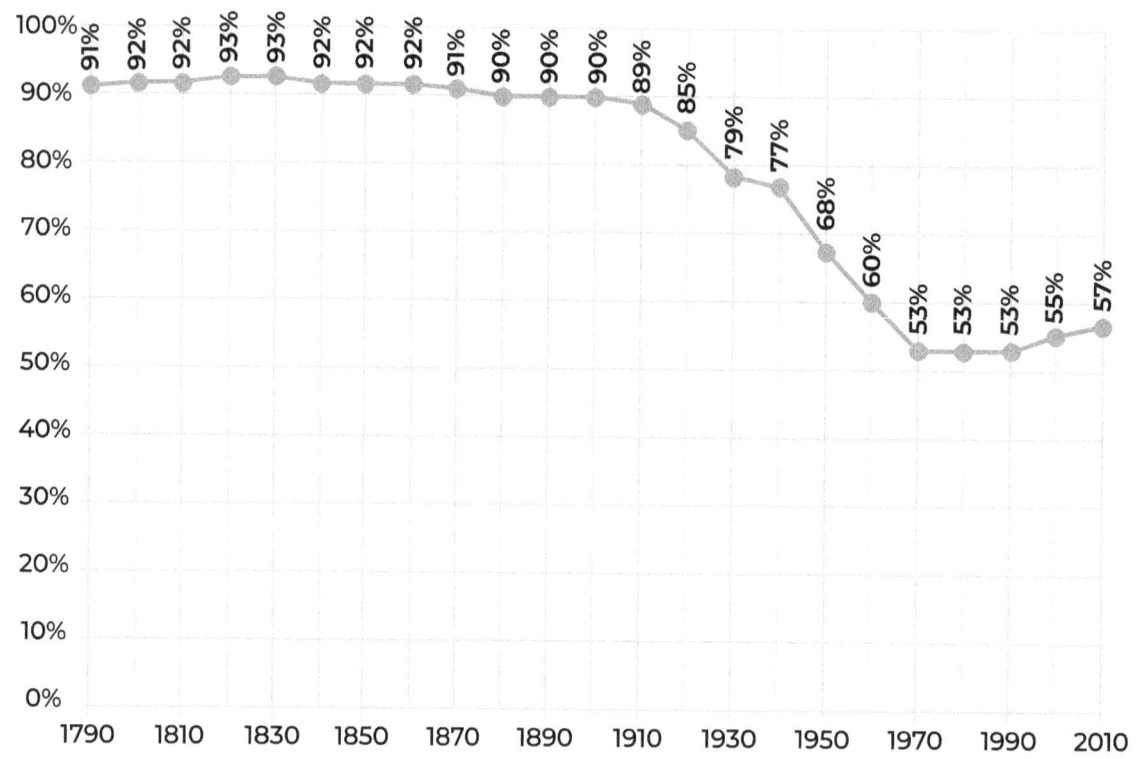

Percentage of African American population living in the American South

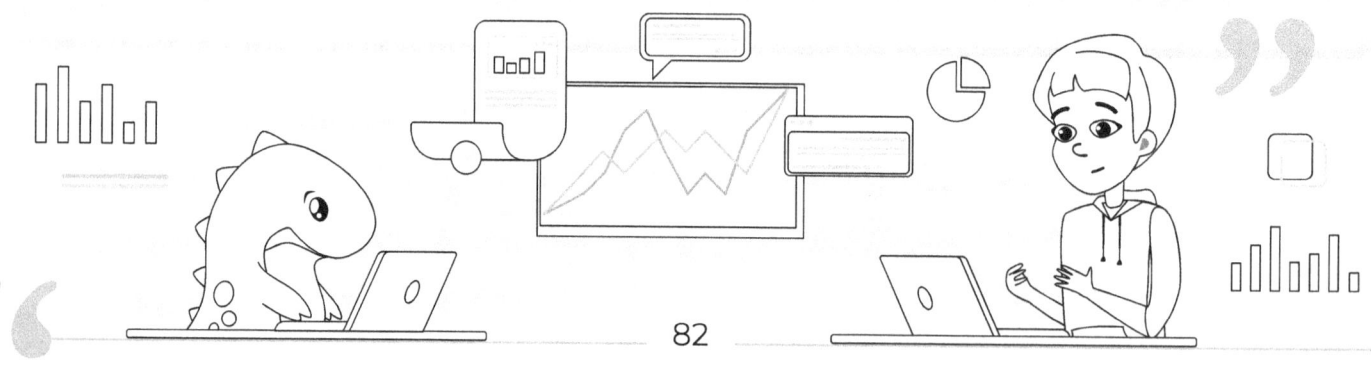

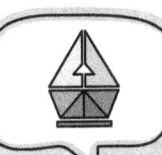
1. Explain the reasons why African Americans would have moved out of the South.

....

....

....

....

2. Describe how the chart in this section explains African American rights issues in the 20th century.

....

....

....

....

3. Explain the reasons why an African American from a rural southern area may be more motivated to move to an urban area.

....

....

....

....

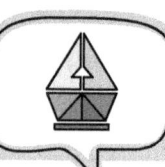
Directions: Read the text below. Then answer the questions that follow.

Both women and African Americans were denied the right to vote in the early 20th century. Women could not vote in many states by law. African Americans were often hindered from voting through Jim Crow laws that established **literacy tests** and **poll taxes** for voters.

1. Why is the right to vote so important?

2. Are there any circumstances today in which you think a person should be denied the right to vote? Explain your reasoning.

3. Certain states have denied the right to vote to convicted felons. What is your opinion on this?

4. What issues today are linked with voting rights?

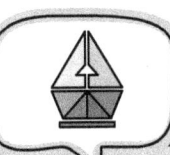
Directions: Read the text below. Then answer the questions that follow.

"

This week, you learned about how women won the right to vote through the 19th Amendment. You also learned about how continued racial discrimination against African Americans in the early 20th century led to violence and the movement of African Americans out of the South.

THE AWAKENING

"

1. Elaborate on how the political cartoon above reflects the struggle for women's suffrage.

....

....

....

....

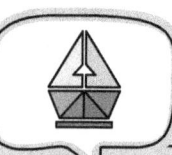
2. In what ways were the fight for women's suffrage and African American rights similar? How were they different?

....

....

....

....

3. This excerpt is from a letter from W.E.B. Du Bois to President Woodrow Wilson in November 1918:

The international peace Congress that is to decide whether or not peoples shall have the right to dispose of themselves will find in its midst delegated from a nation which champions the principle of the "consent of the governed" and "Government by representation." That nation is our own and includes in itself more than twelve million souls whose consent to be governed is never asked. They have no numbers in the legislatures where they are in the majority and not a single representative in the national Congress.

Elaborate on what message Du Bois is telling Wilson.

....

....

....

....

4. A stereotype is a commonly held idea about a particular person or thing that is often overly general or wrong. How might stereotypes of women and African Americans impact changes in law and society?

....

....

....

....

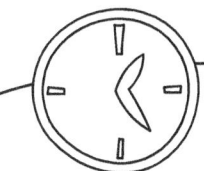

WEEK 9

Economics

The Roaring Twenties and the Stock Market Crash

This week, you will learn about the economy and culture of the 1920s ending with the worst economic crisis in American history.

ARGOPREP

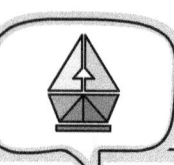
Directions: Read the text below. Then answer the questions that follow.

During the 1920s, the United States entered a period of prosperity. This decade is popularly called the **Roaring Twenties**. These years featured an American constitutional ban on alcohol called **Prohibition** as well as a flowering of popular culture.

The Progressive movement, aside from pushing for reform in industry, government, and politics, also believed that many of society's problems were caused by the drinking of alcohol. A large-scale successful lobbying effort by the **Anti-Saloon League** and the **Women's Christian Temperance Union** resulted in the ratification of the **18th Amendment**, which banned the manufacture and sale of intoxicating liquors in the United States. It went into effect in 1920.

Meanwhile, millions of African Americans were moving from the rural south and into urban areas in the north and midwest. In New York City, many African Americans settled in the neighborhood of Harlem on Manhattan. Harlem drew an array of African American scholars, writers, musicians, and artists. It became a center of culture during what was known as the Harlem Renaissance.

The flourishing of culture was not just limited to Harlem. The 1920s featured the growth of popular culture in film as Hollywood boomed. Radios became a household staple. Jazz grew to prominence, which led the 1920s and some of the 1930s to be called the "**Jazz Age**." Women experienced their own newfound freedoms after winning the right to vote with the ratification of the 19th Amendment. Automobiles became available to the general public with **Henry Ford's** affordable **Model T**. People could now go where they wanted, when they wanted. The suburban areas around cities began to grow as a result. The makings of modern popular culture had emerged.

The Roaring Twenties ended in 1929 with a stock market crash that led to the worst economic crisis in American history, the **Great Depression**.

1. What was a goal of the Women's Christian Temperance Union?

   A. to restrict the expansion of jazz culture

   B. to ban the use of alcohol in the United States

   C. to encourage the growth of the Harlem Renaissance

   D. to fight for women's right to vote

2. What was the Harlem Renaissance?

    A. an economic crash

    B. another name for the 1920s

    C. a flourishing of African American culture

    D. an increase in the number of people living in suburbs.

3. Which of the following did the 18th Amendment do?

    A. banned the manufacture and sale of alcoholic beverages

    B. allowed people's incomes to be taxed

    C. gave women the right to vote

    D. required senators to be directly elected by the people

4. Based on the passage, what is the best explanation as to why suburban areas grew after the introduction of mass-produced automobiles like the Model T?

    A. People worked at factories in the suburbs that produced automobiles.

    B. People saw opportunities to move out of cities and needed automobiles to get to their places of work.

    C. People were attracted to the flourishing culture in the suburbs.

    D. People did not have to rely on public transportation systems to go places so they could live in less dense areas.

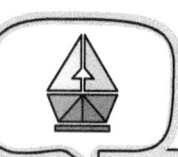
Directions: Read the text below. Then answer the questions that follow.

The Harlem Renaissance generated a number of prominent intellectuals, performers, and writers. The table below shows a handful of the most influential leaders of the Harlem Renaissance in a variety of areas.

Louis Armstrong (1901-1971)

Born in New Orleans, Louis Armstrong was a renowned jazz musician and trumpet player. His work helped make jazz a popular music form and influenced other musicians for decades.

Josephine Baker (1906-1975)

From St. Louis, Josephine Baker witnessed the East St. Louis race riots as a child. She later moved to New York and became a famous dancer and singer on vaudeville and Broadway. In 1925, she moved to France where during World War II she helped gather intelligence for the French resistance.

Countee Cullen (1903-1946)

Countee Cullen was a poet of the Harlem Renaissance. He published his work in many different journals. He first won fame through the publication of "Ballad of the Brown Girl." He published his first collections of poems in the book, *Color*, in 1925. This collection of poems looked at issues of race.

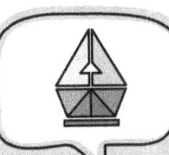

W.E.B. Du Bois
(1868-1963)

W.E.B. Du Bois was a civil rights activist and intellectual who was one of the founders of the National Association for the Advancement of Colored People (NAACP). He was the founder and editor of the organization's magazine, *The Crisis*, which critiqued issues of race in American society.

Langston Hughes
(1902-1967)

Langston Hughes was a poet whose first collection of poetry was published in 1926 under the title *The Weary Blues*. Hughes also wrote novels, plays, and short stories. His work was highly influential on the artistic development of the Harlem Renaissance.

Zora Neale Hurston
(1891-1960)

Zora Neale Hurston was an outspoken leader for African American rights. She is most well known for her novels which depicted life for African Americans.

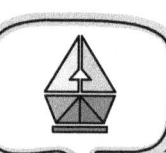
1. Who was known as the editor of *The Crisis*?
   A. Zora Neal Hurston
   B. Josephine Baker
   C. Langston Hughes
   D. W.E.B. Du Bois

2. Which Harlem Renaissance figure is well-known in the area of music?
   A. Louis Armstrong
   B. Countee Cullen
   C. Zora Neale Hurston
   D. W.E.B. Du Bois

3. Who was known as an influential dancer and singer?
   A. Countee Cullen
   B. Zora Neale Hurston
   C. Langston Hughes
   D. Josephine Baker

4. Which of the following people was an influential African American poet and novelist?
   A. Louis Armstrong
   B. W.E.B. Du Bois
   C. Langston Hughes
   D. Josephine Baker

Directions: Read the text below. Then answer the questions that follow.

"

The 18th Amendment prohibited the sale, transport, and making of intoxicating liquors in the United States. The hope was that by stopping people from drinking alcohol, it would lower crime, eliminate poverty, and decrease domestic violence. President Herbert Hoover later described the amendment as "a great social and economic experiment, noble in motive and far-reaching in purpose." To enforce the amendment, Congress passed the **Volstead Act**. It went into effect in 1920.

Immediately, people began to violate Prohibition. As time passed, individuals and organized crime groups made illegal alcohol, which was called bootlegging, and smuggled alcohol into the United States. People who wanted to drink went to secretive saloons, called speakeasies, where they were served liquor. Meanwhile, organized crime began to make immense profits through the illegal trade. The famous gangster **Al Capone** is said to have made $60 million yearly from illegal alcohol sales.

Calls for the repeal of Prohibition gained strength throughout the 1920s. In 1933, the United States ratified the 21st Amendment which repealed Prohibition.

"

1. Explain why Prohibition failed.

_____

_____

_____

_____

2. Explain what the author Robert A. Heinlein meant when he wrote, "Every general prohibition creates its bootleggers."

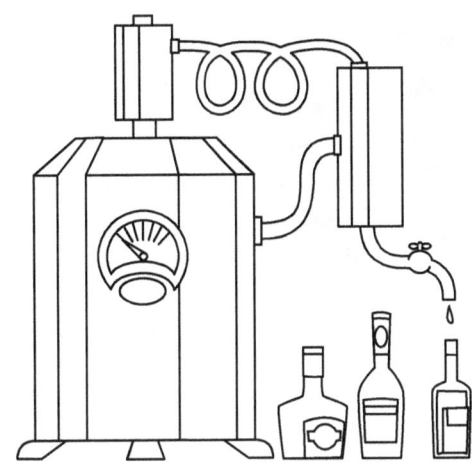

_____

_____

_____

_____

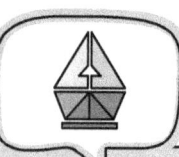
Directions: Read the text below. Then answer the questions that follow.

"

Prohibition lasted from 1920 until 1933. During that time, there was a spike in crime in the United States. Homicides increased throughout the decade and more people were incarcerated. However, there was no decrease in crime until after 1933. While the consumption of alcohol initially dropped at the beginning of Prohibition, by the end of the 1920s it was far higher than it had been before 1920.

"

1. What might be some lessons to learn from America's experience with Prohibition?

....

....

....

....

2. What kinds of recent issues or experiences might relate to Prohibition?

....

....

....

....

Directions: Read the text below. Then answer the questions that follow.

This week you learned about Prohibition and the Harlem Renaissance during the 1920s and their impact on American culture.

1. What might be the importance of the Harlem Renaissance to African American identity based on the experience of Reconstruction and the Jim Crow period?

....

....

....

2. What would someone's main arguments be for repealing Prohibition?

....

....

3. How might Prohibition have impacted an American citizen's trust in government?

....

....

....

4. The 1920s saw new elements of mass or popular culture such as radio, music and movies. What elements of mass culture from the 1920s are shared with us today? What are new elements of mass culture that are different?

....

....

....

....

....

....

....

....

Economics
The Great Depression

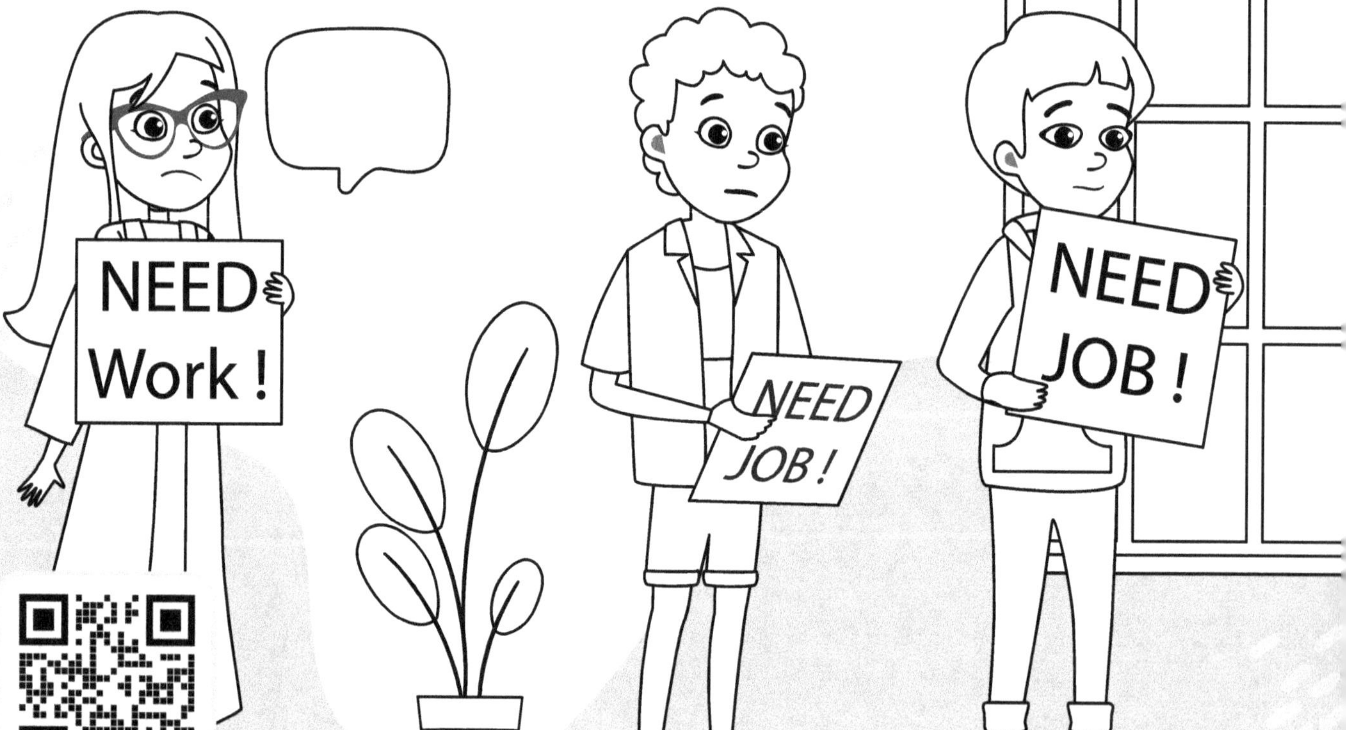

NEED Work !

NEED JOB !

NEED JOB !

This week, you will learn about the Great Depression and its impact on the United States ending with the election of Franklin D. Roosevelt as president.

ARGOPREP

Directions: Read the text below. Then answer the questions that follow.

"

The Great Depression was the worst economic downturn in world history. It lasted from 1929 to 1939. At its worst, in 1933, the United States suffered around a 25% unemployment rate. Approximately 15 million Americans were out of work.

During the 1920s the stock market had greatly expanded with people from all walks of life purchasing shares. People even took out loans to purchase stock, which was called **buying on margin**. They saw it as an easy way to make money and did not think that the value of their stock could go down. People speculated, or took risks, buying up stocks. Prices reached their peak by the fall of 1929. However, the value of the stock was far more than what they were actually worth. In late October, the market crashed as investors panicked and sold off millions of shares of stock. In only a few days, an untold number of people lost their life savings. The economic downturn then spread across the globe.

The situation grew worse as people fell into poverty. Rates of homelessness increased, and people were forced to obtain sustenance from soup kitchens and breadlines. Then as the situation saw no sign of improvement, severe drought coupled with high winds in the Southern Great Plains caused an environmental disaster called the **Dust Bowl**. Confidence in the economy was so broken in the fall of 1930, individuals and companies began to withdraw money from banks in such large amounts that they were forced to shut down.

The Republican President Herbert Hoover did not believe it was the government's role to intervene in the economy nor did he think the government should give economic relief to the country's citizens. Nevertheless, he did offer government loans to businesses and banks.

However, it was not enough, and in the 1932 presidential election, Hoover was beaten by his challenger, Democrat **Franklin Delano Roosevelt** in a landslide. Roosevelt took office in March 1933 and said famously in his inaugural speech, "The only thing we have to fear is fear itself."

"

1. Which of the following was a feature of the Great Depression?

    A. high stock prices

    B. bank closures

    C. people buying shares of stock on loan

    D. low unemployment

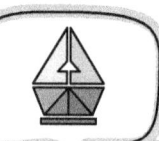

2. Why did people begin to withdraw large amounts of deposits from banks starting in 1930?

   A. People wanted the money to invest in stocks.

   B. People needed the money to fight the Dust Bowl.

   C. People lost confidence in the economy.

   D. People believed that stocks were overvalued.

3. What was the Dust Bowl?

   A. an environmental disaster

   B. an economic disaster

   C. a military disaster

   D. a social disaster

4. What was the cause of the Great Depression?

   A. overspeculation in the stock market

   B. a major drought in the southern Great Plains

   C. high unemployment

   D. bank closures

Directions: Read the text below. Then answer the questions that follow.

One of the most striking features of the Great Depression was the Dust Bowl. The origins of the **Dust Bowl** started in the years after the Civil War when Americans began to settle the Great Plains. As people developed farms in the semiarid southern areas of the plains, they did not account for the environment. Land development intensified in the early 20th century as prices for wheat increased.

When severe drought began hitting in 1930, the overdeveloped land could not hold down the soil. Dust storms occurred as wind tore away topsoil. Millions of acres of land were rendered useless for farming. An unknown number of people died as a result of breathing in so much dust. Dust blew as far east as Washington, D.C. and New York.

The environmental disaster prompted the migration of people away from the region. Nearly 2.5 million people from Oklahoma, Texas, Colorado, New Mexico, and Nebraska fled their homes. Oklahoma was hit particularly hard with over 400,000 people leaving the state. Many of these people fled to California where they were discriminated against as "Okies." This conflict was memorialized in **John Steinbeck's** book, *The Grapes of Wrath*. **Dorothea Lange** took a number of photographs documenting the plight of the people who had been displaced by the dust storms.

The Dust Bowl lasted until 1939 when regular rainfall began to return to the region. However, the Southern Great Plains would take even more years to recover from the environmental disaster.

1. In what geographic region did the Dustbowl occur?

   A. Northeast

   B. Southern Plains

   C. West Coast

   D. Great Lakes

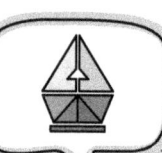
2. What was a cause of the Dustbowl?

    A. migration of people from the Great Plains

    B. the stock market crash

    C. industrial development

    D. overuse of the land for agriculture

3. Which author wrote a book concerning hardships of those impacted by the Dustbowl?

4. Who was Dorothea Lange?

    A. a photographer who took images of people who fled the Dustbowl

    B. a farmer who was displaced by the Dustbowl

    C. a politician who fought for the rights of people who were displaced by the Dustbowl

    D. an author who wrote of the people who fled from the Dustbowl

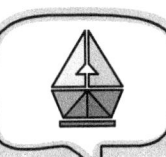
Directions: Read the text below. Then answer the questions that follow.

Graphs and charts help explain historical events in a larger context. Use the graphs below to help explain the impact of the Great Depression. The first chart is a graph of the Dow Jones Industrial Average since 1900. It is a measure of the value of stocks of a certain number of large companies. The second is a graph of the unemployment rate during the Great Depression.

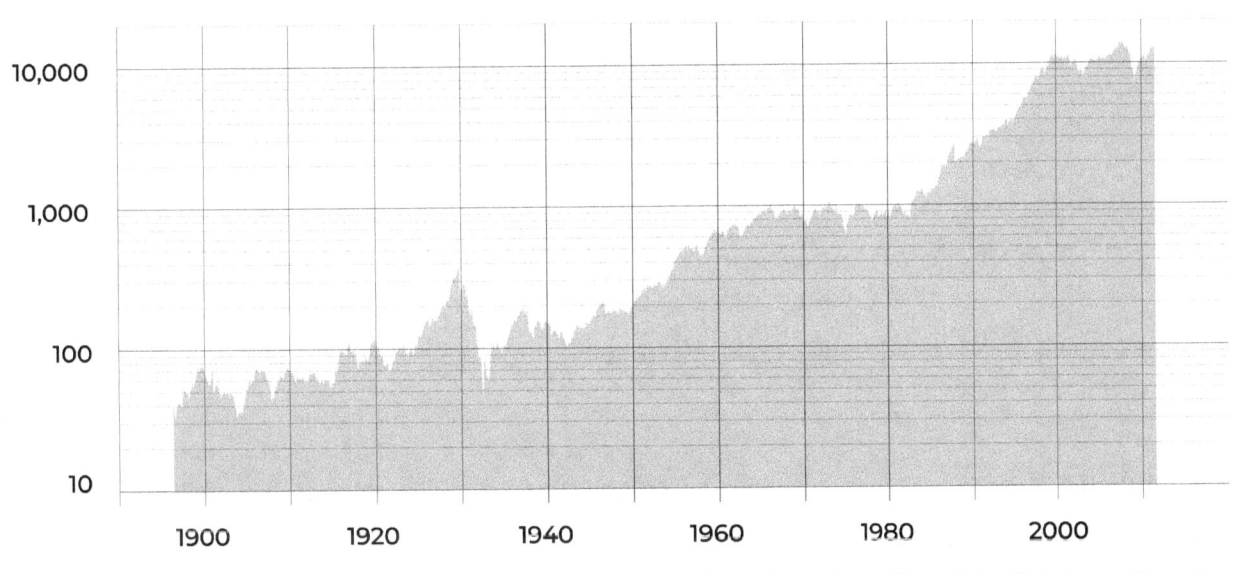

Chart A

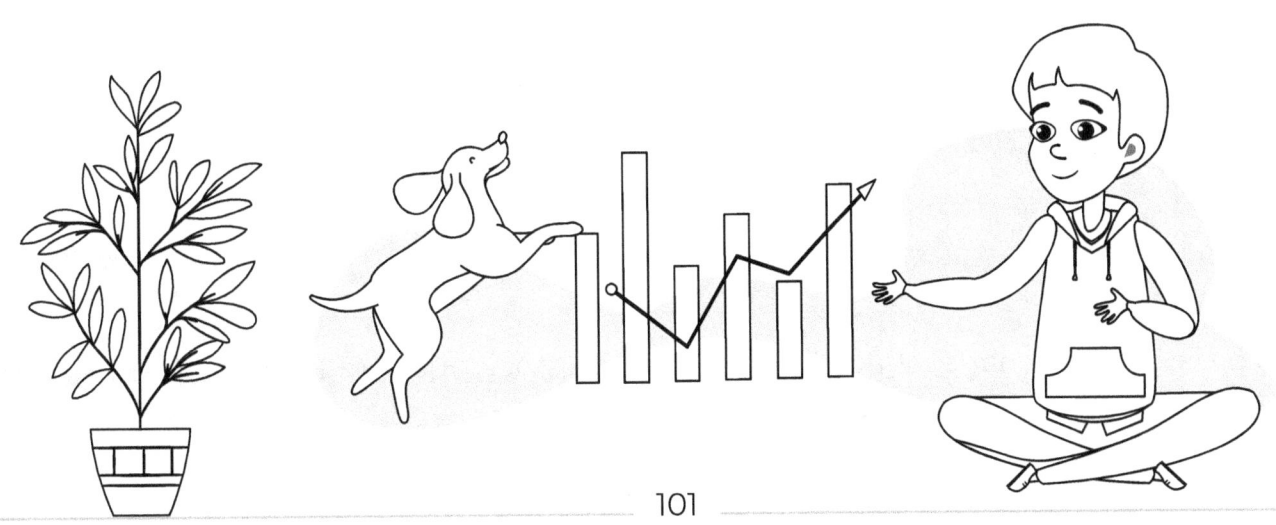

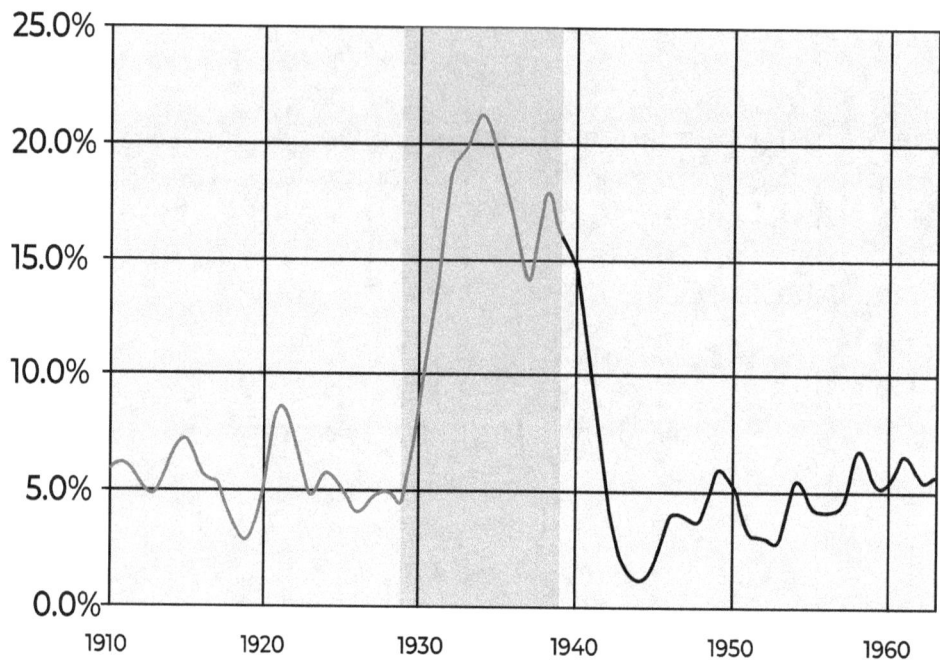

Unemployment rate in the United States, 1910-1960 with the Great Depression years highlighted.

Chart B

1. According to the charts, which year prior to the Great Depression did the Dow Jones Industrial average reach its peak?

2. According to the charts, in about what year did unemployment reach its height during the Great Depression?

3. Which of the two charts show more of the human impact of the Great Depression? Explain why.

4. According to the charts, at about what year did stock prices reach the same prices that they did before the Great Depression?

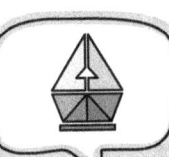
Directions: Read the text below. Then answer the questions that follow.

Imagine yourself as person in the Great Depression who lost all their savings in the Stock Market Crash. There is little prospect in finding a job. Write a letter to a loved one explaining the situation, what your priorities are, and what you think the government should do to help people.

....

....

....

....

....

....

....

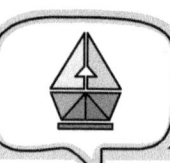
Directions: Read the text below. Then answer the questions that follow.

This week you learned about the causes of the Great Depression and the human suffering that resulted.

1. How might an economic disaster such as the Great Depression bring about change for the good?

....

....

....

....

2. How was the general public partially responsible for the start of the Great Depression?

....

....

....

....

3. In 1932, voters overwhelmingly elected Franklin Delano Roosevelt as president over the incumbent Herbert Hoover. Why would voters elect Roosevelt over Hoover?

....

....

....

....

4. How might the photographs of Dorothea Lange and the works of John Steinbeck help deal with the problems of the Great Depression?

....

....

....

WEEK 11

Civics and Government

The New Deal

This week, you will learn about the policies and programs of the New Deal which were designed to combat the Great Depression.

ARGOPREP

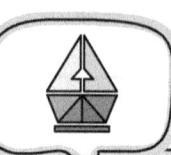
Directions: Read the text below. Then answer the questions that follow.

In 1932, voters elected **Franklin Delano Roosevelt** president in a landslide victory over Herbert Hoover. Citizens had given Roosevelt a mandate to try new policies in order to combat the Great Depression.

When Roosevelt took office in 1933, he worked with Congress to enact multiple pieces of legislation to provide relief from the Great Depression. This was called the **"New Deal."** Most famous were the months following Roosevelt's inauguration called "the first hundred days." Some of the New Deal's most famous programs were enacted at that time.

In order to connect with citizens, Roosevelt began a series of filmed "Fireside Chats." It was through these that the upbeat Roosevelt attempted to restore faith in the country's economy.

However, the Depression continued to drag on. In response, Roosevelt enacted a "Second New Deal" in 1935 which which created more government programs. Conservative critics of the New Deal believed that it was not the government's role to regulate the economy nor provide welfare programs for people. In fact, the Supreme Court started ruling some of the New Deal's programs as unconstitutional. Roosevelt proposed to add more Supreme Court Justices in order to allow his programs to remain in effect. This proved unneeded since soon after Roosevelt's plan became public, the Supreme Court started voting to uphold New Deal programs.

Most historians believe that the New Deal did not end the Great Depression, noting that Roosevelt's programs were not aggressive enough. Instead, they claimed the New Deal blunted the economic disaster. The Great Depression did not end until massive spending was needed for World War II. However, even today, New Deal programs remain such as social security and unemployment insurance.

1. What was the New Deal?

   A. a communication tool used by Franklin D. Roosevelt
   B. a series of programs to fight the Great Depression
   C. a series of criticisms of the Roosevelt administration by the Supreme Court
   D. a time period early in the Roosevelt administration

2. What was an objection by conservative critics of the New Deal?

   A. The government should not regulate the economy.
   B. The government was not using all its powers to fight the Great Depression.
   C. The economy needed intervention.
   D. The economy needed more government spending.

3. Why did Roosevelt propose to add more justices to the Supreme Court?

   A. He believed it would help communicate his message about the New Deal.
   B. He believed that it created more debate.
   C. He wanted more conservative justices to disapprove New Deal programs.
   D. He wanted more liberal justices to approve New Deal programs.

4. What was the legacy of the New Deal?

   A. It successfully ended the Great Depression.
   B. It left government programs still in use today.
   C. It helped cause World War II.
   D. It brought the number of justices in the Supreme Court to its level today.

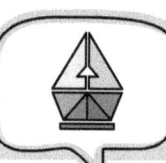
Directions: Read the text below. Then answer the questions that follow.

The New Deal enacted many different programs. These programs, often abbreviated with acronyms, were referred to as an "alphabet soup." The table below describes some of the major laws and programs of the New Deal.

Name	Year Enacted	Description
Agricultural Adjustment Act (AAA)	1933	This law offered subsidies (payments) for not growing certain kinds of crops. Its purpose was to increase and stabilize agricultural products. After being ruled unconstitutional in 1936 by the Supreme Court, a replacement law was passed in 1938 which was then ruled constitutional.
Banking Act	1933	This law instituted the Federal Deposit Insurance Corporation (FDIC) to protect bank deposits. It also separated commercial and investment banking as well as putting in other banking reforms. Several aspects of this law were repealed in later decades, but provisions such as the FDIC still exist.
Civilian Conservation Corps (CCC)	1933	This was a work relief program that was used by men ages 17 to 28. It provided environmental jobs such as planting trees, creating trails, and other tasks that helped create the national and state parks still in existence today. This program ended in 1942.
National Industrial Recovery Act (NIRA)	1933	This law attempted to set prices and wages in various industries by allowing businesses to self-regulate through public hearings. The law was judged unconstitutional by the Supreme Court in 1935.
Social Security Act	1935	This law created the social security system, which provides retirees age 65 and older benefits. This system is still in effect.

Tennessee Valley Authority (TVA)	1933	The Tennessee Valley Authority was created in order to control water courses in the Tennessee Valley. It created cheap electricity through its construction of dams. The TVA is still in existence.
U.S. Securities and Exchange Commission (SEC)	1934	The SEC regulates the stock market and enforces federal law. It is still in effect today.
National Labor Relations Act	1935	Also called the Wagner Act, this law guaranteed the right of most workers to form and join labor unions and collectively bargain.
Works Progress Administration (WPA)	1935	Later renamed the Works Projects Administration, this was a federal works project that hired unskilled laborers to build public works, such as buildings and roads. It was ended in 1943.

1. A trader on Wall Street conducts illegal activity for insider trading of shares of stock. Which body would regulate that activity?

A. TVA

B. WPA

C. CCC

D. SEC

2. What law was passed to ensure that elderly people had some income after they retired from work?

A. National Labor Relations Act

B. Social Security Act

C. Wagner Act

D. Banking Act

3. Which New Deal program was meant to assist farmers?

A. AAA

B. TVA

C. WPA

D. CCC

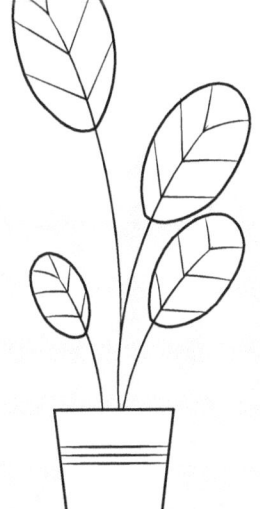

4. Which law guaranteed the right for workers to organize into labor unions?

A. Wagner Act

B. Banking Act

C. Agricultural Adjustment Act

D. Social Security Act

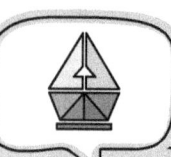
Directions: Read the text below. Then answer the questions that follow.

"

The following passage is an excerpt from a speech by Alfred Landon who ran as the Republican candidate for president against Franklin D. Roosevelt in 1936. Landon lost the race in a landslide victory for Roosevelt:

America has always stood, and now stands, first of all for human rights, for "the life, liberty and pursuit of happiness" of the great Declaration. The prime needs of men have not changed since that Declaration, though new means from time to time may be necessary to meet those needs. But the great safeguards against tyranny and oppression must not be cast away and lost. They must be saved that men may live free to pursue their happiness, safe from any kind of exploitation.

...Our Government was founded to give life to certain vital principles. The people embodied these basic principles of human rights in the Federal and State Constitutions. Thus, the people themselves, of their own free will, set up this Government. And it is still the Government of the people. Any change which the people want they can have by following the procedure they themselves laid down.

But for any official or branch of Government to attempt such a change, without authority from the people, is to do an unwarranted and illegal act. It is a substitution of personal for Constitutional Government. If added power is needed, the people have set out how that authority may be had from them if they wish to give it.

"

1. Based on the passage, explain Alfred Landon's reasons for opposing the New Deal.

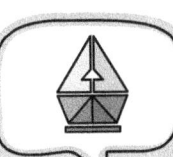
Directions: Read the text below. Then answer the questions that follow.

The New Deal and its programs were the first large-scale intervention of the economy by the federal government in American history. Consider the role government plays in your life when answering the following questions:

1. Which federal programs from the New Deal are still active today?

....

....

....

2. Do you believe that these programs are beneficial? Why or why not?

....

....

....

3. What do you believe is the role of the federal government in people's lives?

....

....

....

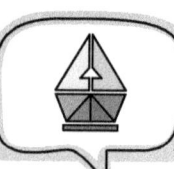
Directions: Read the text below. Then answer the questions that follow.

This week you learned about Franklin Delano Roosevelt and the New Deal. You also learned about some of the New Deal programs that are still in existence today.

1. How did the New Deal help to improve the country's infrastructure?

2. How were labor relations impacted by the New Deal?

3. What aspects of the New Deal were most successful? What aspects were not?

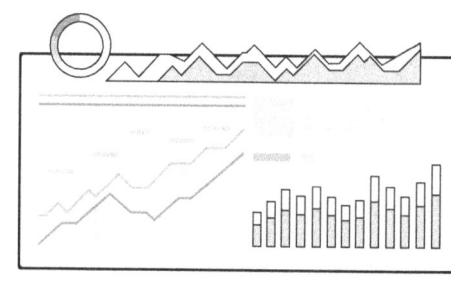
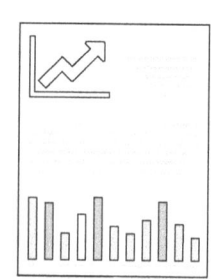

WEEK 12

Geography
World War II

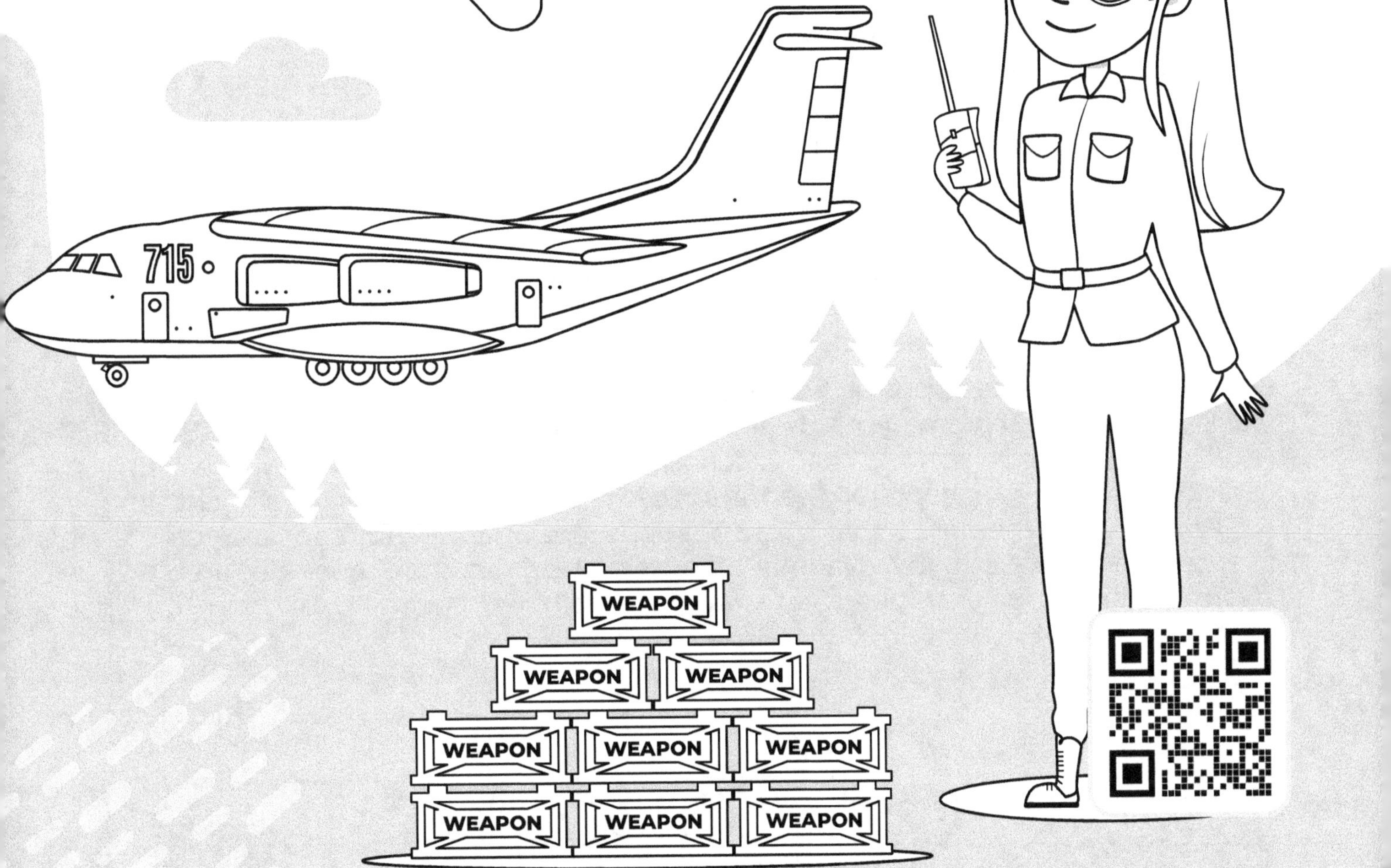

This week, you will learn about the causes of World War II and how the United States became involved in the war.

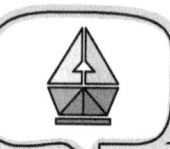
Directions: Read the text below. Then answer the questions that follow.

World War II was the largest and most deadly conflict in human history. With over thirty countries involved in massive fighting around the globe between 1939 and 1945, the war resulted in close to 75 million deaths.

There were several causes of World War II:

* World War I ended with the Treaty of Versailles which placed blame upon Germany for starting the war, including the payment of reparations to the Allies. The reparations crashed Germany's economy leading to instability which led to the rise of totalitarian rule under **Adolf Hitler** and the Nazi Party in 1933. Hitler wanted revenge for the Treaty of Versailles.

* Militarism - Countries turned more to military and totalitarian rule to deal with problems. In Italy, **Benito Mussolini** and the Fascist Party took control in the aftermath of World War I. Japan was led by a military government that was looking to expand its power overseas in order to control natural resources. This led to Japan invading China in 1937.

* Economic - The Great Depression had created economic instability throughout the globe.

* Political - The League of Nations was established after World War I to promote peace. However, it was relatively weak, especially since the United States refused to join the organization.

After Hitler came to power, he began to aggressively expand Germany based on a racist ideology that prominently persecuted Jews. Germany first annexed Austria in 1938 and shortly after demanded that Czechoslovakia be given to Germany. Great Britain, France, and other nations followed a policy of appeasement, giving Czechoslovakia to Germany on the hopes that this would end the potential for conflict. However, in September 1939, Germany invaded Poland. Great Britain and France declared war on Germany. Although the United States would remain neutral until 1941, World War II had begun.

Second World War
1939 - 1945
75 million deaths

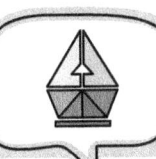
1. How did the Treaty of Versailles help lead to World War II?

    A. The treaty limited the natural resources countries like Germany could have, making them want to expand their borders.

    B. The treaty was an example of an appeasement strategy which failed against totalitarian rulers.

    C. The treaty placed a harsh debt upon Germany which created resentment and economic instability.

    D. The treaty caused a global depression which destabilized governments.

2. How can economic depression help lead to the rise in totalitarian rule?

    A. It can destabilize governments, allowing totalitarian rulers to take power.

    B. It can create a lack of natural resources, forcing countries to go to war with others.

    C. It leads to a policy of appeasement where countries give up important things to maintain the peace.

    D. It is a factor that is not dealt with in global organizations such as the League of Nations.

3. What was a political cause of World War II?

    A. appeasement

    B. reparations

    C. militarism

    D. racism

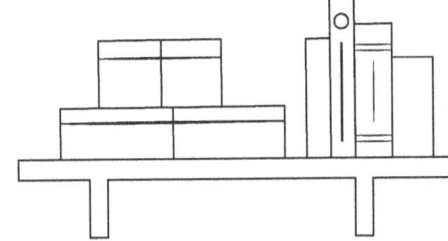

4. Why did Japan seek to expand its territory in the 1930s?

    A. Japan was seeking to create a neutral border around itself.

    B. Japan was seeking natural resources.

    C. Japan was seeking more land to settle people.

    D. Japan was following a policy of appeasement.

Directions: Read the text below. Then answer the questions that follow.

The opposing forces in World War II were divided into two groups, the **Allies** and the **Axis**. The main Axis powers were Germany, Italy, and Japan. The main Allied powers were Great Britain and France who were later joined by the United States and the Soviet Union.

In the early years of World War II, the United States was neutral, but it favored the Allies. After France was conquered by Germany in 1940, Roosevelt declared the United States the "arsenal of democracy" and began shipping military supplies to the Allies under a **lend-lease** program. In this program, the United States lent arms to countries whose defense was deemed vital to U.S. interests with the understanding that they would be paid later. Meanwhile, the war expanded as Germany invaded the Soviet Union in June 1941, breaking a non-aggression pact the two countries signed before the war started. The Soviet dictator Joseph Stalin joined the Allies. The United States also joined the Allies after Japan launched a surprise attack against the American naval base in **Pearl Harbor**, Hawaii on December 7, 1941.

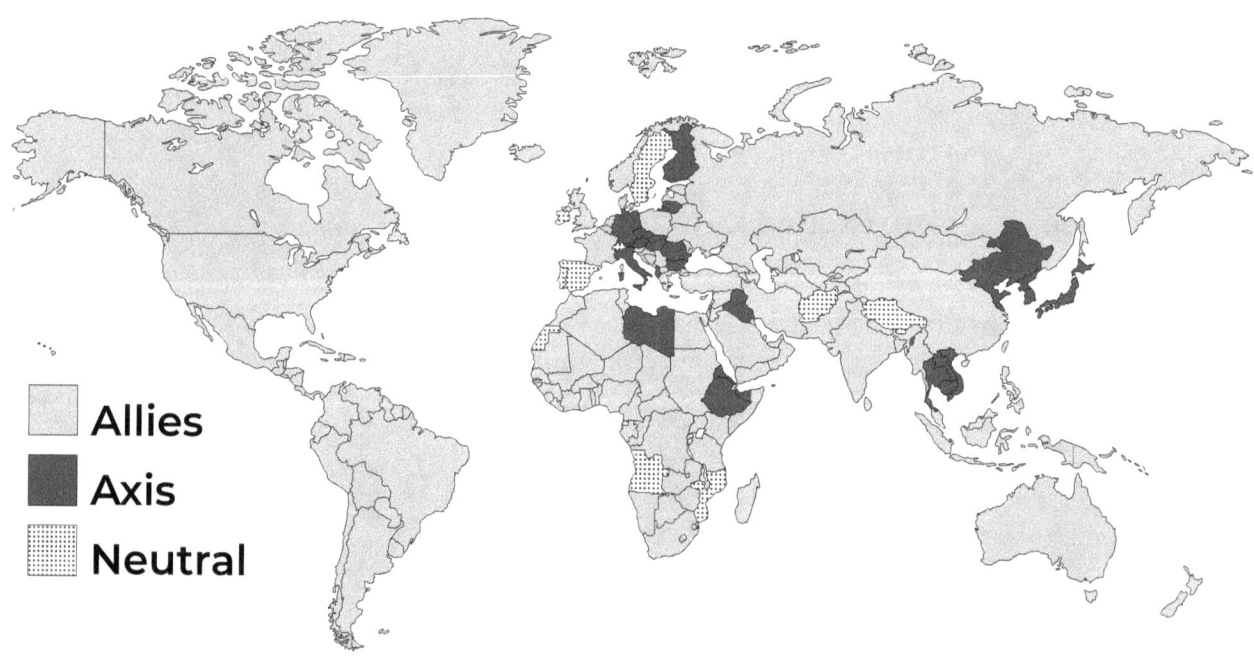

Allies

Axis

Neutral

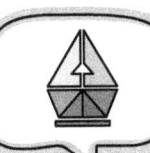
1. The U.S. policy which gave military supplies to Allied nations with the understanding that the country would be paid back later was called _____.

2. According to the map in this section, the _____ countries had the largest amount of land territory.

3. Why might some Americans hesitate to become involved in World War II?

....

....

....

....

4. The attack on _____ drew the United States into World War II on the _____ side.

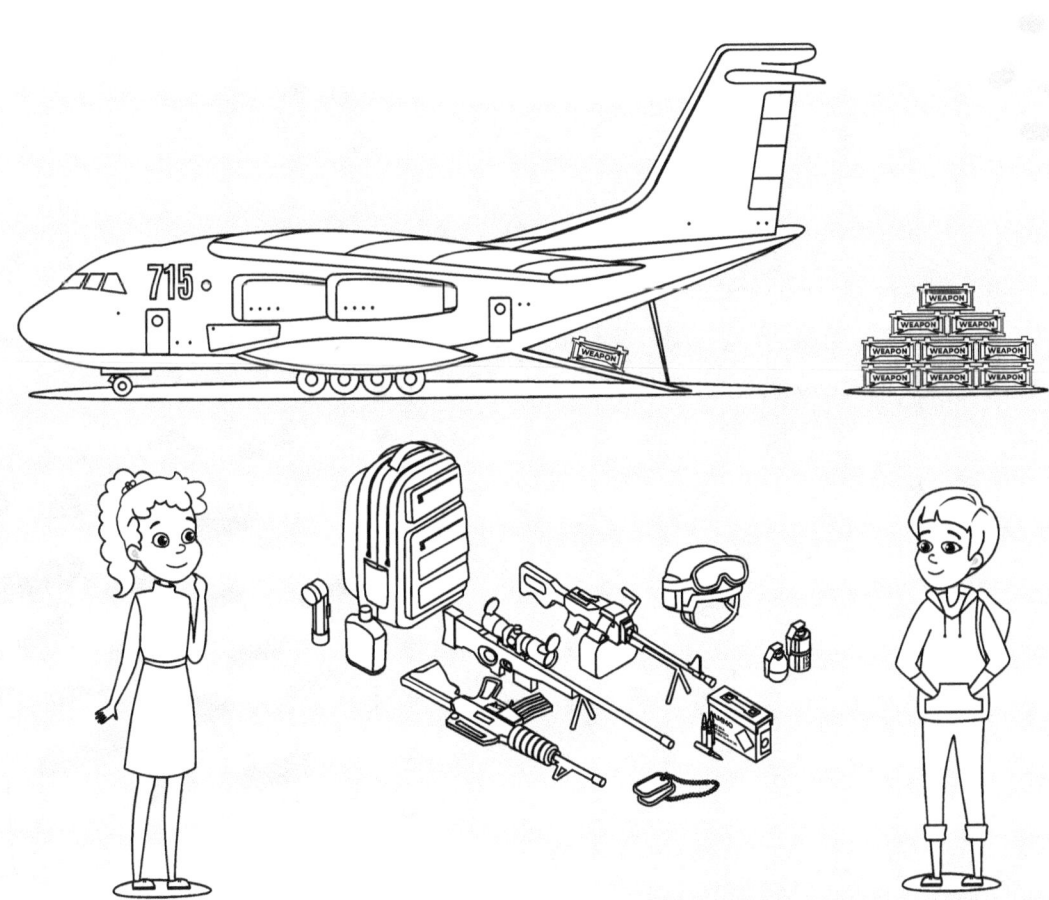

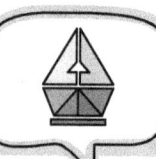
Directions: Read the text below. Then answer the questions that follow.

World War II was fought not only in the Pacific and in Europe but also at home. The war transformed the American economy and brought it out of the Great Depression. Also, with well over 12 million men going abroad to serve as soldiers, women filled occupations traditionally filled by men. Women worked in factories assembling military equipment and supplies. The women's labor force grew by about 6.5 million. A symbol of the importance of women's contributions to the war effort was **"Rosie the Riveter"** who was modeled on women who worked in the country's factories to produce war materials. Women also were in the military service, with 350,000 in uniform in noncombat, supporting roles like the **Women's Army Corps (WAC).**

1. Explain how World War II may have helped women's rights.

....

....

....

2. Explain what reaction the artist of the cartoon in this section is trying to get from the viewer. Who do you think the cartoon is meant for?

....

....

....

....

....

....

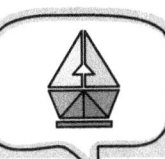
Directions: Read the text below. Then answer the questions that follow.

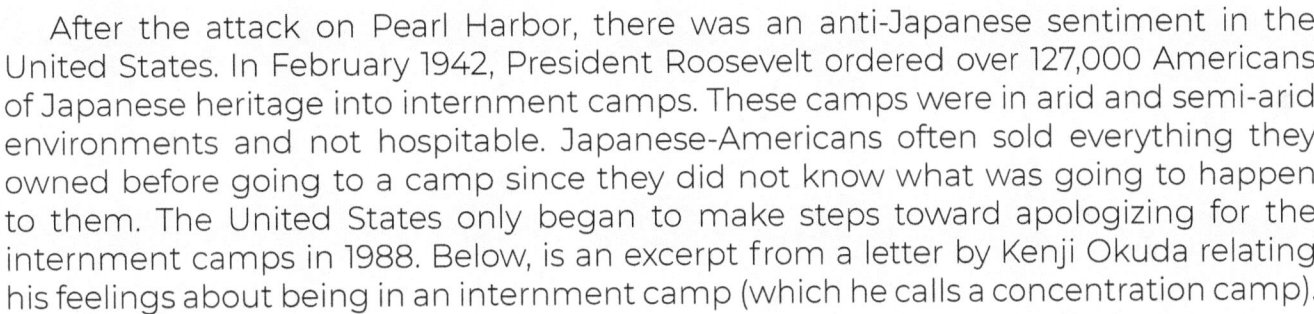

After the attack on Pearl Harbor, there was an anti-Japanese sentiment in the United States. In February 1942, President Roosevelt ordered over 127,000 Americans of Japanese heritage into internment camps. These camps were in arid and semi-arid environments and not hospitable. Japanese-Americans often sold everything they owned before going to a camp since they did not know what was going to happen to them. The United States only began to make steps toward apologizing for the internment camps in 1988. Below, is an excerpt from a letter by Kenji Okuda relating his feelings about being in an internment camp (which he calls a concentration camp).

Dear Norio-san,   *May 30, 1942*

On this first Memorial Day after our fateful entrance into a frightening, devastating war.... Thousands of young Americans have already perished and other thousands are fighting furiously dying and killing.... There is nothing in this camp to remind us of that occasion except a memorial service this evening at 7. No military parade will we see; no valiant half-hearted display of armed might.... Just a quiet service for those Japnese pioneers who have died striving that we, their children, might inherit something of that Great American ideal, Democracy.

But how futile and hypocritical this all sounds... in concentration camps in a <u>Democracy</u>... to be kept herein at the sole discretion of the military.... And yet to be willing to do our best to insure the defeat of a nation with which so many of us are connected only by racial and racial characteristics.

1. What points is Kenji Okuda making in his letter about the nature of democracy and the United States?

....

....

....

2. How might you feel if you were sent to an internment camp based on your racial identity?

....

....

....

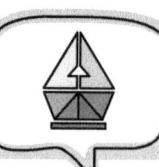
Directions: Read the text below. Then answer the questions that follow.

This week you learned about the causes of World War II. You also also learned about the contributions of women to the war effort, as well as the internment of Japanese Americans during the war.

1. How are World War I and World War II linked?

....

....

....

....

2. How did the spending needed for World War II help lead to the end of the Great Depression?

....

....

....

....

3. How was the treatment of Japanese Americans during World War II comparable to the treatment of other groups in American history?

....

....

....

....

....

....

Geography

Fighting World War II and Its Aftermath

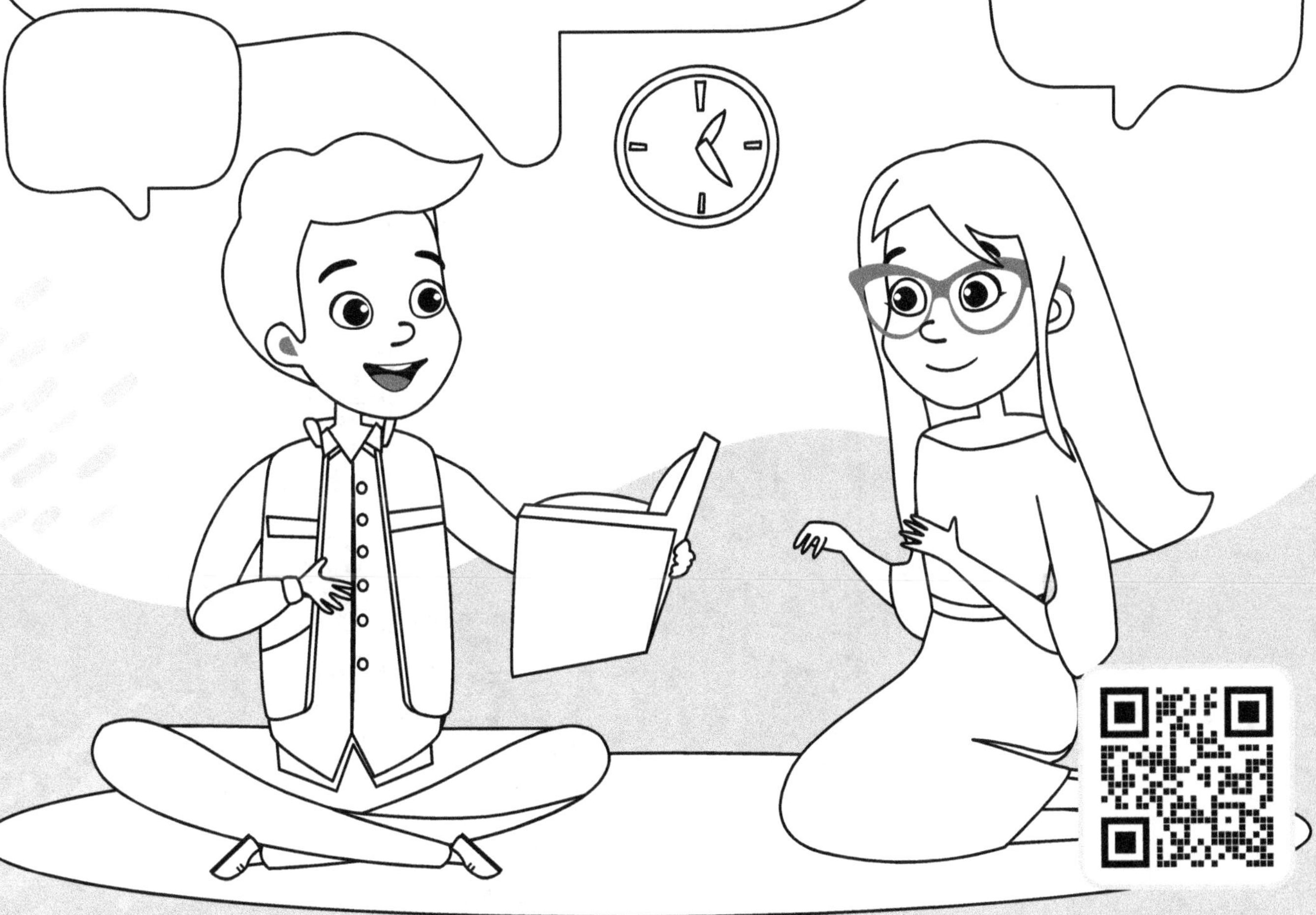

This week, you will learn about how World War II was fought, how it ended, and how it impacted the world.

ARGOPREP

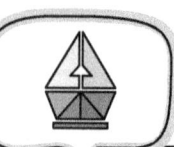
Directions: Read the text below. Then answer the questions that follow.

World War II was fought on many fronts. In Europe, Germany expanded and controlled most of the continent by 1942 using fast moving military tactics known as **blitzkrieg** which means "lightning war." In the Pacific, Japan extended its empire until it had control over much of East Asia and the Pacific.

However, the war turned against the Axis powers that same year. In Europe, Adolf Hitler gambled everything on being able to conquer the Soviet Union quickly. He lost that gamble, and starting in 1942, the Soviets began to drive the Germans back with heavy losses. Meanwhile, in June 1942, the Japanese suffered a major loss to the American fleet at the **Battle of Midway**. The American military was then able to push Japan back through the use of an "island-hopping" strategy in which U.S. forces would cut off Japanese bases by skipping ahead to islands further in. In 1944, the Allies staged an invasion of occupied France known as **D-Day**. After that, it was obvious the Allies were going to win the war, but it took another year of fighting and the use of nuclear bombs against Japan to bring a final victory.

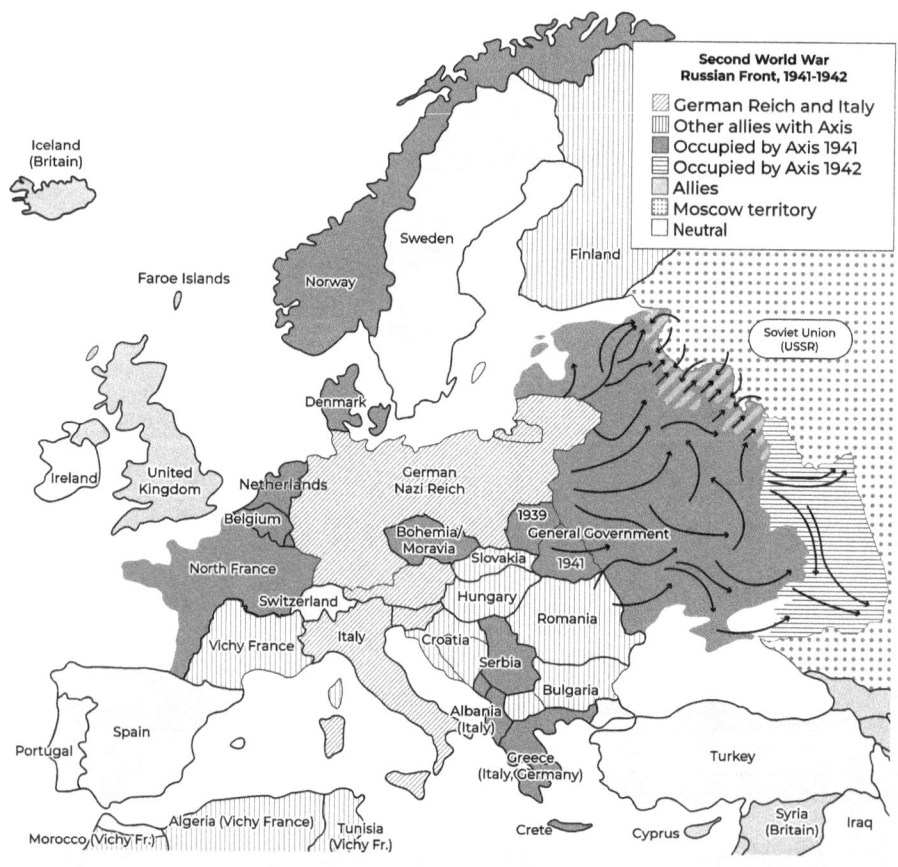

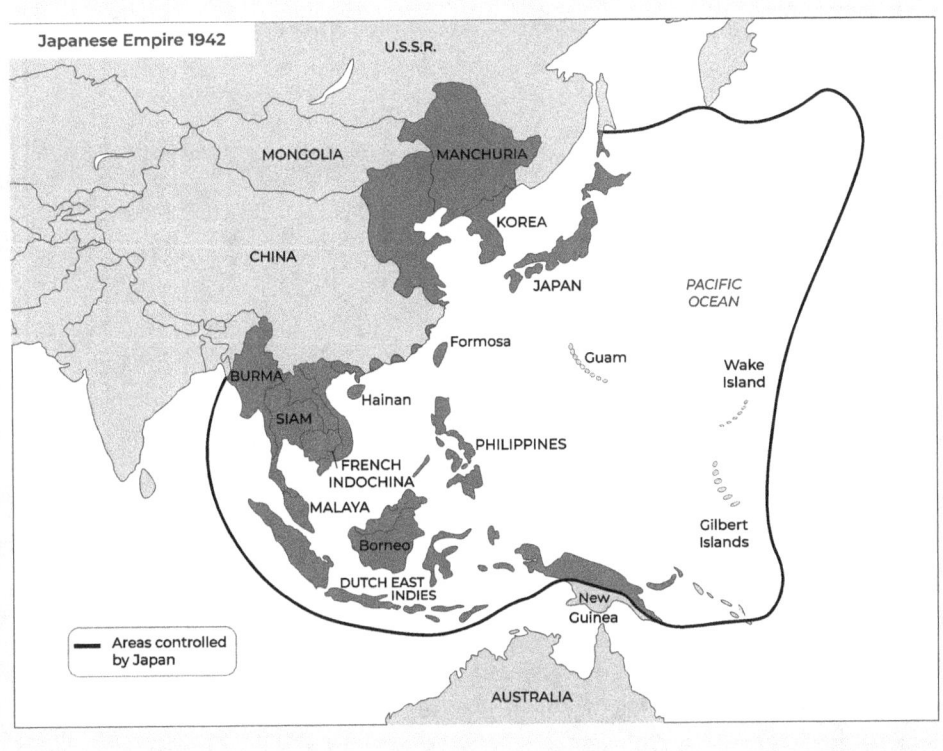

1. What was the Battle of Midway?
   A. a defeat of Japanese forces by the United States
   B. a defeat of German forces by the Soviets
   C. an invasion of France by the Allies
   D. a battle in which nuclear weapons were used against Japan

2. What was the farthest eastern extent of Germany's conquests during World War II?
   A. Africa
   B. Norway
   C. France
   D. Soviet Union

3. Which of the following countries was neutral during World War II?
   A. France
   B. Spain
   C. United Kingdom
   D. Japan

4. During World War II, _____ conquered the Philippines.
   A. Germany
   B. Italy
   C. Japan
   D. Soviet Union

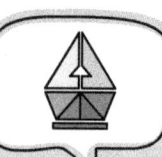
Directions: Read the text below. Then answer the questions that follow.

During World War II, not only did military personnel die in unparalleled numbers but also civilians. Some of the worst cases of genocide, or the mass murder of a group, occurred during the war. Most prominently was the attempted extermination of Jewish people by Nazi Germany, as well as the mass killing of civilians by Japan.

In Germany, Nazis blamed Jews for many of the world's problems, claiming that they were an inferior race. During the war, approximately six million Jews and five million others including Romani and Poles, were murdered at death camps such as Auschwitz and Dauchau. This amounted to about two-thirds of the entire population of European Jews. This mass-killing is known as the **Holocaust**.

In Asia, Japanese military forces killed civilians on a large scale. At Nanjing, China, for example, some estimates show that nearly 300,000 people were killed by the Japanese military in 1937. Similar killings to a lesser scale occurred throughout Asia during the war.

At the end of the war, the victorious Allies held **war crime trials** in Nuremberg and Tokyo. It was there that the world learned the full horror of the violence of the war. In part, these tragedies led to a call for international unity and the creation of the **United Nations**.

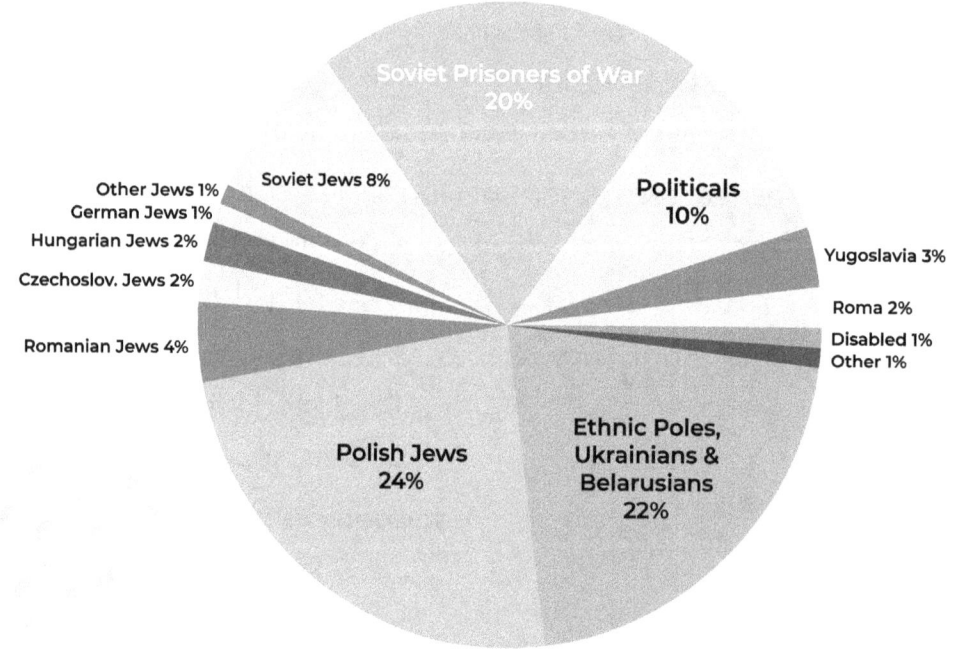

Holocaust Deaths

1. The killing of six million Jews and five million other people in Europe by the Nazis is called _____.

2. _____ is the mass killing of a group of people.

3. In which city were war crime trials conducted?

    A. Nuremberg

    B. Berlin

    C. Amsterdam

    D. Beijing

4. Why would the war crime trials after World War II lead to calls for an international organization like the United Nations?

....

....

....

....

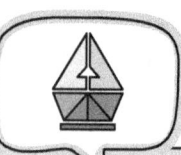
Directions: Read the text below. Then answer the questions that follow.

"

During World War II, the leaders of the three largest of the Allied powers met several times to discuss the future of the world after the war. These men were known as the **"Big Three."** The first was U.S. President Franklin D. Roosevelt who was replaced by **Harry Truman** after his death in 1945. The second was Prime Minister **Winston Churchill** of Great Britain who was replaced by Clement Attlee in 1945. The third was Soviet dictator **Joseph Stalin**.

"

August 1941	At the **Atlantic Conference** Roosevelt met with Churchill while the United States was still neutral and established the **Atlantic Charter,** agreeing to no territorial changes after the war, the right for people to realize self-determination, and the idea of an international organization to keep world peace. This idea became the United Nations.
January 1943	At the **Casablanca Conference** Churchill and Roosevelt agreed that Germany must unconditionally surrender to the Allies.
November 1943	At the **Tehran Conference**, Stalin, Roosevelt, and Churchill discussed a strategy against Germany, and Stalin promised that the Soviet Union would enter the war against Japan once Germany was defeated.
February 1945	At the **Yalta Conference**, the Big Three agreed that Germany would be occupied in different zones. In addition, Roosevelt and Churchill agreed that governments friendly to the Soviet Union would be allowed along the Soviet border in exchange for free elections in those countries. That promise was not kept, and Stalin installed communist rule in Eastern European countries after the war
July 1945	At the **Potsdam Conference**, Atlee, Truman, and Stalin discussed the future of Germany and demanded the unconditional surrender of Japan. During the conference, Truman received news that the United States had successfully conducted a test of an atomic bomb.

1. Explain how Allied strategy was developed at the Tehran Conference.

....

....

....

....

2. Considering the events of World War II, explain why the Soviet Union may want countries with friendly governments along its border.

....

....

....

....

3. Explain how the Atlantic Conference set the stage for the creation of international cooperation.

....

....

....

....

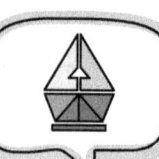
Directions: Read the text below. Then answer the questions that follow.

Throughout World War II, the United States raced to develop an atomic bomb through a large scale project called the Manhattan Project. In July 1945, the first atomic bomb was successfully tested. Meanwhile, Japan showed no sign of surrender. Truman needed to decide what to do. He could choose a conventional bombing of Japan. In prior bombing campaigns, hundreds of thousands had been killed. He could also order an invasion of Japan by ground forces. Estimates of casualties could be in the millions. He could also choose to use the atomic bomb.

In August 1945, President Harry Truman authorized the use of atomic bombs against the Japanese cities of Hiroshima and Nagasaki. The bombings occurred on August 6th and 9th killing upward of 200,000 people. Japan surrendered on August 15, 1945.

1. If you were President Truman, what choice would you make? Explain.

....

....

....

2. Some have felt that Truman's decision was the equivalent of a war crime. What is your thinking on this?

....

....

....

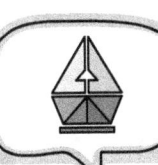
Directions: Read the text below. Then answer the questions that follow.

This week you learned about the fighting and end of World War II.

1. Joseph Stalin was a dictator of the Soviet Union while Franklin Roosevelt and Winston Churchill were the heads of democracies. How might these differences impact the peace after World War II?

....

....

....

....

2. Elaborate on how the events of World War II helped lead to the creation of the United Nations.

....

....

....

....

3. The Big Three agreed that they would concentrate on defeating Germany before Japan. What could be the reasons why the Big Three would agree on this strategy?

....

....

....

....

WEEK 14

History
The Cold War

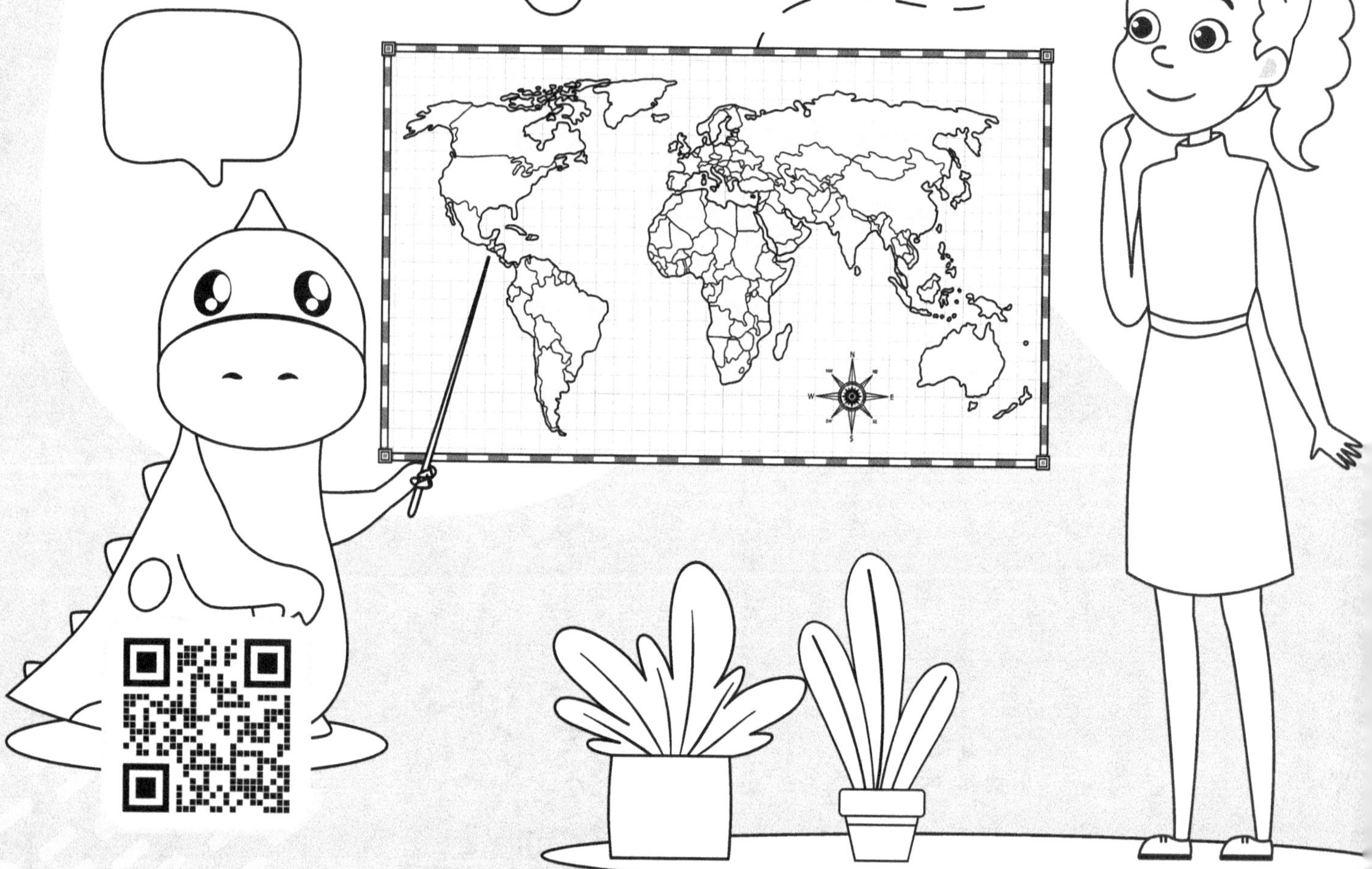

This week, you will learn about the origins and tensions of the Cold War, the rivalry between the Soviet Union and the United States after World War II.

Directions: Read the text below. Then answer the questions that follow.

After World War II, the world divided politically into three different groups. The first were those aligned with the United States and its allies. This alliance, created in 1949, was called the **North Atlantic Treaty Organization** (NATO). The countries in NATO were generally democracies with capitalist economic systems. NATO also had a number of countries allied to it. The second group was comprised of those countries that aligned themselves with the Soviet Union in an alliance called the **Warsaw Pact,** which was established in 1955. These countries were communist countries with totalitarian governments. One exception to this was China, which was communist but was not allied with the Soviet Union. The third group was comprised of those countries that did not ally with either the Warsaw Pact or NATO. This period of division is called the **Cold War** because there was no open "hot" conflict like in World War II.

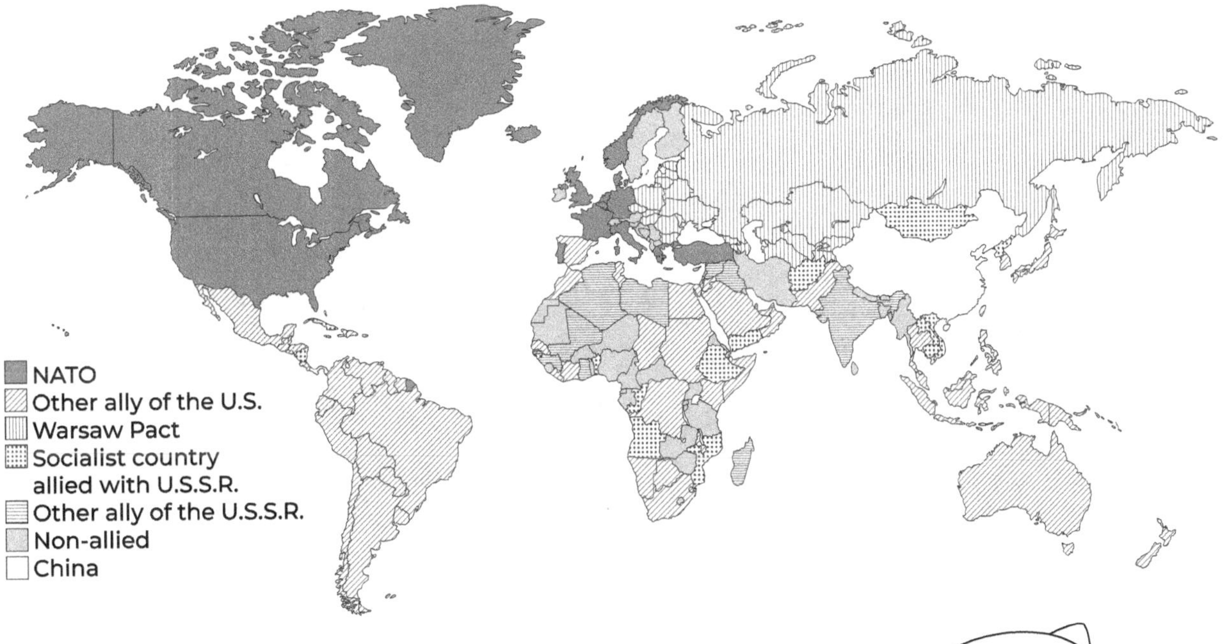

- NATO
- Other ally of the U.S.
- Warsaw Pact
- Socialist country allied with U.S.S.R.
- Other ally of the U.S.S.R.
- Non-allied
- China

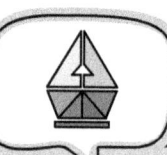
1. Members of the North Atlantic Treaty Organization generally had what kind of government?

   A. communist

   B. democratic

   C. totalitarian

   D. socialist

2. According to the map, members of the Warsaw Pact were located in

   A. North America

   B. Northern Africa

   C. South America

   D. Eastern Europe

3. According to the map, which geographic area was most closely aligned with the United States?

   A. Western Hemisphere

   B. Eastern Hemisphere

   C. Northern Hemisphere

   D. Southern Hemisphere

4. Which country, while communist, did not ally itself with the Soviet Union?

   A. Poland

   B. East Germany

   C. China

   D. Vietnam

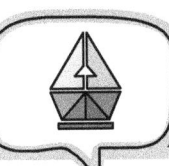
Directions: Read the text below. Then answer the questions that follow.

> The Cold War lasted from 1947 until 1991. During the Cold War, the world was **bipolar** which means that the majority of world power was held by two countries. Before the Cold War, the world was **multipolar,** with many countries holding power. During the Cold War, the two strongest countries were the United States and the Soviet Union. They were so much more powerful that they were also called **superpowers**.
>
> Part of the reason for this power was that both sides had nuclear weapons. As the Cold War advanced, both countries became involved in a nuclear **arms race** with each side building more and more weapons. The escalation of weapons increased tensions between the countries so much that they nearly came to war.
>
> The United States followed a strategy of **containment**. This strategy tried to keep communism from spreading to other countries. This strategy also brought the United States into wars in Korea (1950-1953) and Vietnam (1955-1975). The competition between the two superpowers also resulted in the **Space Race** in which the Soviet Union launched the first man, Yuri Gagarin, into space in 1961, and the United States landed the first human, Neil Armstrong, on the moon in 1969.
>
> The Cold War ended between 1989 and 1991 when the economies of the Soviet Union and its allies collapsed. The countries of Eastern Europe replaced their governments with non-communist ones, and the Soviet Union broke apart into other countries. The world after the Cold War became **unipolar** with only one superpower, the United States.

1. What is containment?

   A. It was the limiting of nuclear arms after the Cold War.

   B. It was a strategy used by the United States during the Cold War to contain the spread of communism.

   C. It was a competition between the United States and Soviet Union during the Cold War.

   D. It was a term to describe the global world order during the Cold War.

2. In which country was a war fought by the United States to fight communism?

   A. Soviet Union

   B. East Germany

   C. Korea

   D. China

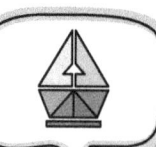
3. According to the passage, what might have been a benefit of the Cold War?

....

....

....

....

4. Why did the Cold War end?

   A. NATO won a war against the Warsaw Pact.

   B. The Vietnam War brought an end to the conflict.

   C. A treaty was signed, ending the war.

   D. The economies of communist countries collapsed.

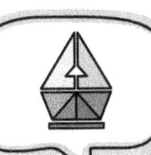
Directions: Read the text below. Then answer the questions that follow.

Part of the reason why the Soviet Union and the United States did not go to war was because of nuclear weapons. Nuclear weapons were so powerful that it was thought that if one country went to war with the other, then both would be destroyed. This reasoning was called **mutually assured destruction**. Both countries built enough nuclear weapons to destroy the other side several times over.

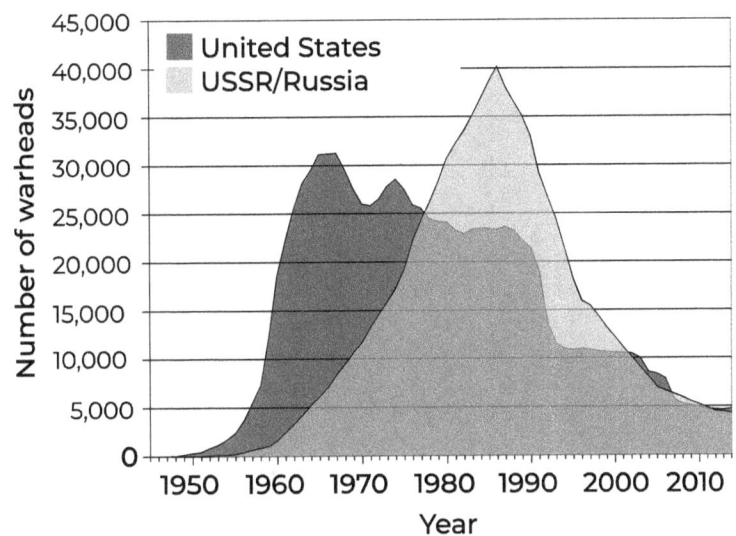

The closest the superpowers came to war was during the **Cuban Missile Crisis** in October 1962. The Soviets were installing nuclear missiles on the island of Cuba which is only about 70 miles away from the continental United States. The United States, led by President John F. Kennedy, blockaded the island. Tensions cooled when the two countries made an agreement that the Soviet Union would not install the missiles if the United States removed its nuclear weapons from Turkey.

1. Explain how mutually assured destruction works.

....

....

....

....

2. Looking at the chart in this section, explain the trend in nuclear arms growth during the Cold War.

....

....

....

3. Explain how the Cuban Missile Crisis came to an end.

....

....

....

....

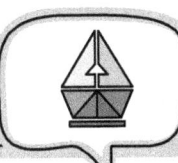
Directions: Read the text below. Then answer the questions that follow.

1. Nuclear war was a global threat that people worried about the most during the Cold War. List three other global threats that exist now. Do you think they are more dangerous than nuclear war?

_____

_____

_____

_____

2. Draw a political cartoon or write a poem describing the idea of mutually assured destruction during the Cold War.

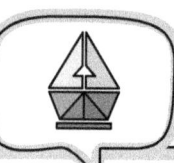
Directions: Read the text below. Then answer the questions that follow.

This week you learned about the Cold War. Based on your reading, respond to the following questions.

1. The Space Race was one beneficial outcome of the Cold War. What might have been others? Elaborate on your reasoning.

_____

_____

_____

_____

_____

2. Is the world multipolar, unipolar, or bipolar today? Elaborate on your reasoning.

_____

_____

_____

_____

_____

3. Could the Cold War have been avoided? Why or why not?

_____

_____

_____

_____

_____

WEEK 15

Economics

Post-War America

This week, you will learn about the post-war boom in the United States and changes to the country demographically.

ARGOPREP

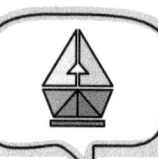
Directions: Read the text below. Then answer the questions that follow.

After World War II, the United States entered a period of prosperity and growth. Thousands of veterans returned home and benefited from a new law nicknamed the **G.I. Bill** which provided education and loans for housing assistance. Veterans took advantage of these loans and began to settle down. Families grew. In the immediate decades after the war, the birthrate spiked in what is called the **baby boom**.

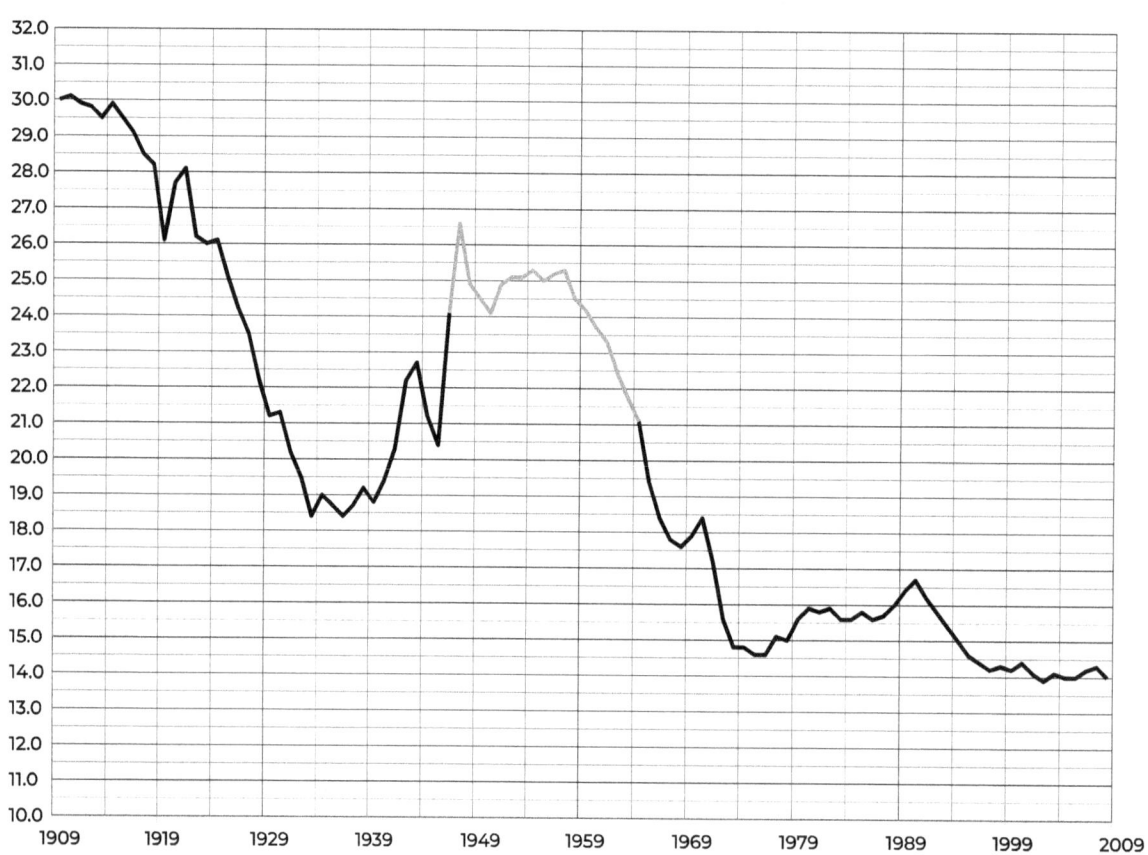

The growing number of children demanded a growth in schools and services. The baby boom generation became a dominant group of people beginning in the middle of the twentieth century. By the 1960s, about 40 percent of the American population were baby boomers. This spike in population numbers helped the American economy from toy production to automobiles as the baby boomers aged. However, as this population ages and passes into retirement, they are likely to put a strain on the economy and impact social security.

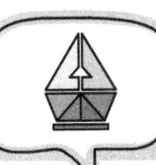
1. What was the baby boom?

    A. It was a growth in the building of schools after World War II.

    B. It was the rise in prosperity after World War II.

    C. It was a spike in birth rates after World War II.

    D. It was the uptick in education after World War II.

2. Why would an aging baby boom population strain resources and social security?

    A. It is such a large population group, and smaller population groups will be responsible for them financially.

    B. Consumer demand declines with age.

    C. The post-war country did not account for changes in population.

    D. There will be an oversupply of goods produced for baby boomers.

3. According to the graph, in approximately what year of the baby boom were birthrates the highest?

    A. 1910

    B. 1948

    C. 1970

    D. 1950

4. What was something the G.I. Bill provided?

    A. well-paying jobs

    B. social security

    C. tuition assistance

    D. free homes

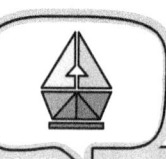
Directions: Read the text below. Then answer the questions that follow.

Another big change after World War II was that people began to move out of cities and into suburbs. Like the baby boom, suburbia grew because of post-war prosperity, the help of the G.I. Bill, and affordable housing. People saw the opportunity to own a home, and because automobiles were affordable, they relied on commuting to jobs via cars rather than public transportation.

The first post-war suburban project was Levittown on Long Island, New York which was developed by **William J. Levitt**. These homes were pre-fabricated, and the town was planned so that it could be built rapidly. This made the homes affordable. Levittown was very successful, and similar suburbs developed throughout the country outside of large cities. However, there was a dark side to Levittown. Levitt refused to sell houses to people of color, and buyers had to sign agreements called covenants that claimed they would not sell their homes to people of color. This established a segregated community. This practice was found to be illegal.

While the growth of suburbs helped keep the economy prosperous, it also created problems. Suburbs impacted the environment as more people used cars than ever before. Natural environments were destroyed for land development. Also, as people left cities, the cities began to fall into urban decay - a term used to describe the deterioration of a city typically due to lack of funds- as tax revenue shrunk. As conditions in cities worsened, more people left them for the suburbs. Another part of this problem was that more white Americans were leaving cities in a phenomena called **"white flight."** This created a division between suburban America and its cities. This also brought to many people's attention the racial injustices that had long troubled the country.

1. Why were houses in Levittown cheaper?

   A. because they were manufactured in advance

   B. because buyers received help from the G.I. Bill

   C. because there was greater demand than supply

   D. because its location allowed easy access to jobs

2. How would a reduction in the amount of tax revenue lead to urban decay?

....

....

....

3. How did William J. Levitt's policy impact civil rights issues in the United States?

_____

_____

_____

_____

_____

_____

4. Do you think the growth of suburbia was primarily good or bad for the United States? Explain why.

_____

_____

_____

_____

_____

_____

_____

Directions: Read the text below. Then answer the questions that follow.

"

As the country grew in the post-war years, it slowly became aware of people's impact on the environment. Since the industrial revolution, years of damage started to become apparent. This problem was brought to the attention of the public through Rachel Carson's book *Silent Spring* which documented how pesticides were harming the environment. Her book helped to give rise to the modern environmental movement as well as the establishment of the **Environmental Protection Agency** in 1970.

One terrible environmental disaster happened in Niagara Falls, New York in a neighborhood named **Love Canal**. This area was the site of a chemical waste dump between 1942 and 1953. In the 1970s, these chemicals leached into the soil, causing birth defects, cancers, and other diseases. Families had to be evacuated from their homes. This disaster forced the government to intervene in 1980 with a law nicknamed the **Superfund** to clean up environmentally damaged sites.

People also began to recognize how animal species were being impacted by human activity. In the 20th century, several species were nearing extinction due to habitat loss, pollution, poaching, and other human activities. This even included the bald eagle, the symbol of the United States. In response, Congress passed the **Endangered Species Act** in 1973. The law has been generally successful, although human pressures continue to make the recovery of species difficult.

"

1. Explain how disaster leads to positive change.

....

....

....

....

2. Explain how the growth of settlement patterns into suburban areas can harm environments.

....

....

....

....

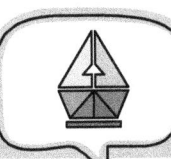
Directions: Read the text below. Then answer the questions that follow.

> William J. Levitt was the developer who built multiple Levittowns around the country after World War II. He enforced racial segregation in these towns. He wrote, "'The Negroes in America are trying to do in 400 years what the Jews in the world have not wholly accomplished in 600 years. As a Jew, I have no room in my mind or heart for racial prejudice. But... I have come to know that if we sell one house to a Negro family, then 90 or 95 percent of our white customers will not buy into the community. This is their attitude, not ours. As a company, our position is simply this: We can solve a housing problem, or we can try to solve a racial problem, but we cannot combine the two."

1. What do you think is Levitt's purpose behind what he wrote?

....

....

....

....

....

....

2. Do you think what Levitt predicted was correct? Do you think that prediction would be correct now? Explain your reasoning.

....

....

....

....

....

....

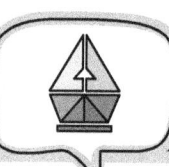
Directions: Read the text below. Then answer the questions that follow.

1. Consider where you live. Is it a suburb, a town, a city, or a rural area? Describe where you live and then conduct some research. Describe what your area was like geographically one hundred years ago.

2. The baby boom was an important event in American history. How are you connected to the baby boom? How is it still impacting you?

Civics and Government

The Civil Rights Movement

This week, you will learn about the Civil Rights Movement and how it impacted the country politically and socially.

ARGOPREP

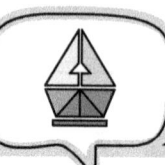
Directions: Read the text below. Then answer the questions that follow.

In the decades after World War II, the United States began to face the long unresolved issues of racial inequality. As you may recall, in the years after the Civil War, African Americans were freed from slavery but their rights were suppressed through Jim Crow laws. These laws required poll taxes and literacy tests for the right to vote. African Americans, who due to racist practices were poor and often illiterate, could neither afford to pay the tax nor pass a literacy test. Segregation of whites and African Americans pervaded in large areas of the country. From schools, to different seating zones on buses, to water fountains, people of color could not use white facilities. These laws were found constitutional by the Supreme Court in 1896 in the case **Plessy v. Ferguson** which claimed that separate facilities were allowable, stating that they needed to be "**separate but equal**." However, there was hardly any equality.

The first major step toward racial equality occurred after World War II when President Harry S. Truman desegregated the military with Executive Order 9981 in 1948. However, segregation remained the law of the land until the landmark **Brown v. Board of Education of Topeka** in 1954. In this case, the Supreme Court overturned Plessy v. Ferguson declaring that "separate but equal" was unconstitutional. Still, many people did not accept the outcome of the case. This set the stage for the Civil Rights movement of the 1960s.

1. What did *Plessy v. Ferguson* rule?

   A. that racial segregation was constitutional

   B. that poll taxes were unconstitutional

   C. that literacy tests for voting were constitutional

   D. that the president's desegregation of the military was unconstitutional

2. How did a poll tax stop African Americans from voting?

   A. Only whites were allowed to pay the tax.

   B. African Americans often could not afford to pay it.

   C. The tax paid for white-only voting facilities.

   D. African Americans often could not read.

SEPARATE BUT EQUAL

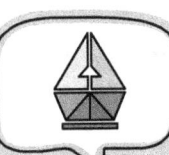
3. What is an example of segregation?

    A. a poll tax which suppresses African American voting rights

    B. a literacy test which African Americans cannot pass

    C. a school designated for African Americans only

    D. a bus where all races can sit in any seat

4. What is the most likely reason President Harry S. Truman issued Executive Order 9981?

    A. He saw the problems of segregated schools.

    B. He saw the contributions of African American veterans in World War II.

    C. He saw how poll taxes were suppressing African Americans' right to vote.

    D. He had to comply with the *Brown v. Board of Education of Topeka* decision.

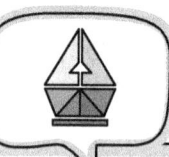
Directions: Read the text below. Then answer the questions that follow.

In 1951, **Oliver Brown**, an African American, filed a class-action lawsuit against the Board of Education in Topeka, Kansas for not allowing his daughter to attend the nearby whites-only school. Brown was represented by the National Association for the Advancement of Colored People (NAACP) who merged the case with several others.

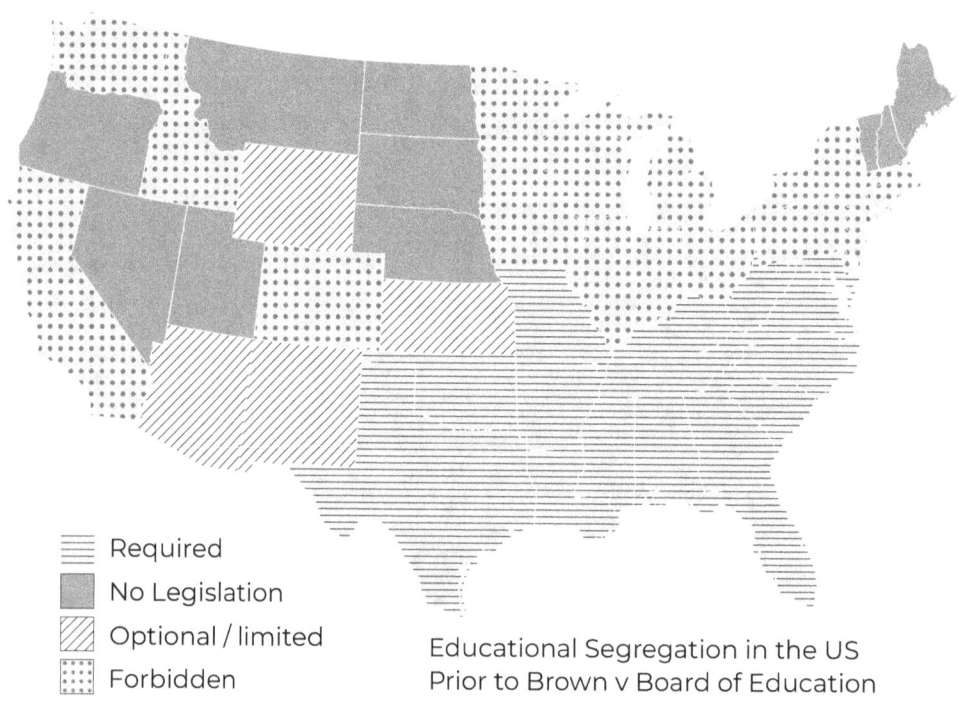

Required

No Legislation

Optional / limited

Forbidden

Educational Segregation in the US
Prior to Brown v Board of Education

The NAACP was trying to overturn "separate but equal." Brown and the others were represented by **Thurgood Marshall** of the NAACP. Marshall was later appointed as the first African American Supreme Court justice in 1967 by President **Lyndon B. Johnson**. The case went before the Supreme Court, headed by Chief Justice **Earl Warren**. The court in 1954 unanimously ruled that segregation was unconstitutional since it violated the equal protection clause under the Fourteenth Amendment, which states that no state can "deny to any person within its jurisdiction the equal protection of the laws." The court ordered that the country desegregate with "all deliberate speed." This prompted segregationists to organize. The era of civil rights protests had begun.

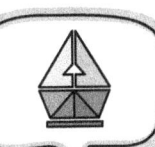
1. Who represented the plaintiff in *Brown v. Board of Education of Topeka*?

   A. Earl Warren

   B. Oliver Brown

   C. Lyndon B. Johnson

   D. Thurgood Marshall

2. According to the map, which region of the country required African Americans and whites to have separate facilities?

   A. Northeast

   B. Southeast

   C. Northwest

   D. Midwest

3. What timeline did the Supreme Court give states to desegregate facilities?

   ....

   ....

   ....

4. How was the Fourteenth Amendment used in *Brown v. Board of Education of Topeka?*

   ....

   ....

   ....

STOP RACISM

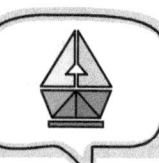
Directions: Read the text below. Then answer the questions that follow.

Timelines are used to explain when events occur in sequence so a person may have a better understanding of history. The timeline below contains some of the chief events of the early years of the civil rights movement.

1948   President Harry S. Truman desegregates the military.

1954   In *Brown v. Board of Education of Topeka*, the Supreme Court headed by Chief Justice Earl Warren overturns *Plessy v. Ferguson*.

1955   Rosa Parks refuses to give up her seat to a white man on a segregated bus in Montgomery, Alabama. This sparks the Montgomery bus boycott.

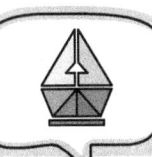

1957

President Dwight D. Eisenhower sends troops to Little Rock, Arkansas to enforce the desegregation of Little Rock High School.

1961

Black and white civil rights activists ride segregated buses in what are called the "Freedom Rides." They are met with violence.

1963

Reverend Martin Luther King, Jr., a central figure in the civil rights movement who advocated nonviolent protests, gives a famous speech before the Lincoln Memorial known as the "I Have a Dream Speech" during the March on Washington.

1964

President Lyndon B. Johnson signs into law the Civil Rights Act of 1964. This law bars employers from discrimination based on race, color, sex, religion, or national origin. This is followed up in 1965 by the Voting Rights Act which makes literacy tests as a voting requirement illegal.

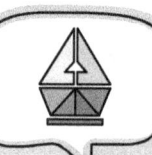

1965

Police brutally attack protestors marching from Selma to Montgomery, Alabama. Images of the violence help to gain support for the 1965 Voting Rights Act which makes literacy tests as a voting requirement illegal. This same year, the black religious leader and civil rights activist Malcolm X is assassinated.

1968

Martin Luther King, Jr. is assassinated in Memphis, Tennessee. That same year, Lyndon Johnson signs the 1968 Fair Housing Act which makes discrimination in housing illegal.

1. Based on the timeline, what generalizations can you make about the Civil Rights movement?

....

....

....

2. On this timeline, which event do you think sparked the civil rights movement? Why?

....

....

....

....

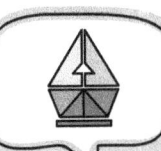
Directions: Read the text below. Then answer the questions that follow.

Reverend **Martin Luther King, Jr.** was an advocate of nonviolence. He was influenced by the successful protests of Mohandas Gandhi in India in achieving independence from Great Britain. He was also greatly influenced by Christian ideas of nonviolence.

Contrasting to King was **Malcolm X** who was born as Malcolm Little. He, like King, experienced firsthand racism and wanted an end to it. Unlike King, however, Malcolm X advocated for racial separation and advocated for freedom "by any means necessary," not ruling out the use of force.

1. Based on your reading, which form of protest do you think is more effective? Malcolm X's or King's? Explain your reasoning.

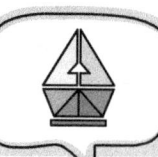
Directions: Read the text below. Then answer the questions that follow.

This week you learned about the Civil Rights Movement. Consider your reading as you answer the following questions:

Lyndon B. Johnson signing the 1964 Civil Rights Act with Martin Luther King, Jr. looking on.

1. In what ways was the Civil Rights Movement most successful?

....

....

....

2. What issues from the Civil Rights Movement are still being debated today?

....

....

....

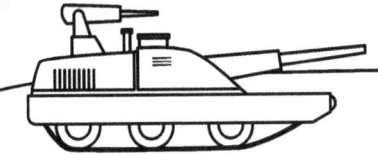

WEEK 17

History
The Vietnam War Era

 This week, you will learn about the Vietnam War era, America's involvement in the war, and the passage of legislation to improve civil rights and fight poverty.

ARGOPREP

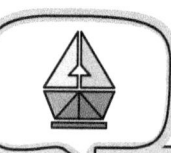
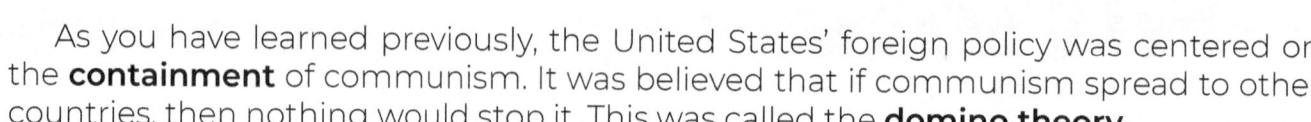

Directions: Read the text below. Then answer the questions that follow.

As you have learned previously, the United States' foreign policy was centered on the **containment** of communism. It was believed that if communism spread to other countries, then nothing would stop it. This was called the **domino theory**.

France once controlled an area called French Indochina, which are known as the countries of Vietnam, Laos, and Cambodia today. In 1954, Vietnamese rebels defeated French troops at the battle of **Dien Bien Phu**. Vietnam was divided into two parts, with communists under **Ho Chi Minh** in control in the North.

The United States first became involved in the Vietnam War under Presidents Dwight D. Eisenhower and John F. Kennedy by sending military advisors, arms, and aid to South Vietnam. However, the war escalated in 1964 under President Lyndon Johnson. Meanwhile, the Soviet Union continued to send military assistance to North Vietnam. Soon, U.S. troops were directly involved in combat.

Vietnam was a highly divisive war in the United States. Many people believed that Americans should be directly involved in the war to fight communism. Many others objected to the war. There was a growing peace movement which objected to the **conscription** of young men to fight in an overseas war through the draft. By 1967, there were 500,000 troops in Vietnam. In 1968, the North Vietnamese launched the **Tet Offensive** which, while not militarily successful, nevertheless stirred more antiwar sentiment in the United States.

As casualties mounted, President Johnson declared in 1968 that he would not run again for office. That year, Richard M. Nixon won the presidency. Nixon, controversially bombed neutral Cambodia where there were communist bases. Slowly, the United States withdrew its troops until the last left in 1975. Vietnam by then was entirely controlled by the communists. Over 58,000 Americans had died.

1. What was Dien Bien Phu?

   A. a battle that the French lost

   B. a North Vietnamese leader

   C. a military campaign

   D. a South Vietnamese leader

2. Which president escalated the war in Vietnam?

   A. Lyndon B. Johnson

   B. Richard Nixon

   C. John F. Kennedy

   D. Dwight D. Eisenhower

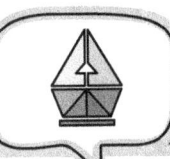
3. What was a reason why many young people protested the war in Vietnam?

    A. They supported Ho Chi Minh.

    B. They thought the United States needed to send more troops.

    C. They felt that containment was wrong.

    D. They objected to the draft.

4. What was the impact of the Tet Offensive?

    A. It signaled the end of French imperialism in Southeast Asia.

    B. It bolstered the growing peace movement in the United States.

    C. It was a major military victory for North Vietnam.

    D. It resulted in the immediate evacuation of American troops.

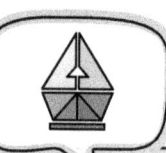
Directions: Read the text below. Then answer the questions that follow.

The 1960s were a period of great change in the United States, in part because of protest against the Vietnam War, but also because of the influence of the Civil Rights Movement. A **counterculture** developed in the United States which coincided with the years of the Vietnam War.

The counterculture rejected many traditional societal norms and is best represented by the image of the **hippie**. Embracing the peace movement and civil rights, the counterculture listened to different forms of music, fought for women's rights, partook in drugs, and sought sexual liberation. Music provided a key means of spreading the counterculture, with music groups such as the Beatles, the Doors, and Rolling Stones reaching the peak of their popularity. A famous music

festival in **Woodstock**, New York became a cultural touchstone for the period.

The counterculture ended at nearly the same time as the Vietnam War. Much of the reason for this is that the movement achieved its goals of progress for civil rights and the end of the war. Also, many of the elements of the counterculture became absorbed into American mainstream culture.

1. How was the counterculture linked to the Vietnam War?

....

....

....

2. The counterculture embraced more than a rejection of the Vietnam War. How can the embrace of new philosophies be explained in light of other events of the era?

....

....

....

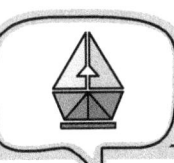
Directions: Read the text below. Then answer the questions that follow.

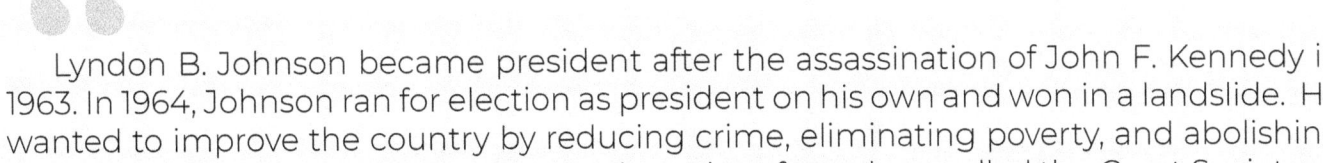

"

Lyndon B. Johnson became president after the assassination of John F. Kennedy in 1963. In 1964, Johnson ran for election as president on his own and won in a landslide. He wanted to improve the country by reducing crime, eliminating poverty, and abolishing racial discrimination. Johnson proposed a series of new laws called the Great Society.

The Great Society included the **Civil Rights Act of 1964** and the **Voting Rights Act of 1965** which aimed to reduce discrimination in places of work and eliminated literacy tests as a voting requirement. It also included numerous other laws and programs that are still in use today. Much of this was to wage Johnson's initiative on the "War on Poverty." Some of the most prominent features of the War on Poverty included:

* **Medicare** which provides assistance with health care costs of the elderly and disabled.

* **Medicaid** which provides assistance with health care costs of the impoverished.

* **Head Start** which provides educational assistance to low-income families.

* **The Elementary and Secondary Education Act** which provides assistance to low-income school districts.

* **The Economic Opportunity Act** which created an Office of Economic Opportunity to provide job assistance to the unemployed.

However, the War on Poverty suffered as the Vietnam War escalated. The federal government was forced to shift more and more funding to the war effort and away from Johnson's programs. As a result, Johnson did not run for office again. Instead, in 1968, Republican candidate **Richard M. Nixon** became president, riding on a wave of anger and resentment toward the war and the Great Society.

"

1. Explain how the Vietnam War and the Great Society were linked.

....

....

....

....

....

....

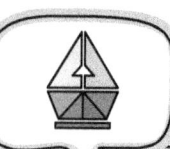
2. The Great Society contained some landmark legislation. Explain how the landslide victory by Johnson in 1964 enabled it.

_____

_____

_____

_____

3. Why might people have been against Great Society laws and programs?

_____

_____

_____

_____

_____

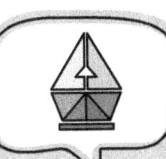
Directions: Read the text below. Then answer the questions that follow.

"

President Lyndon Johnson had to make a choice between spending federal funds on Great Society programs or on the Vietnam War. This type of choice is sometimes called **"Guns versus Butter."** Guns in this case represent the national defense and butter represents spending on domestic programs. You only have a limited amount of funds to devote to one thing or another.

Imagine you are the president of the United States today and have to choose between spending for national defense versus investing in domestic improvements. What choices would you make? How would you divide the funds? Explain your reasoning.

"

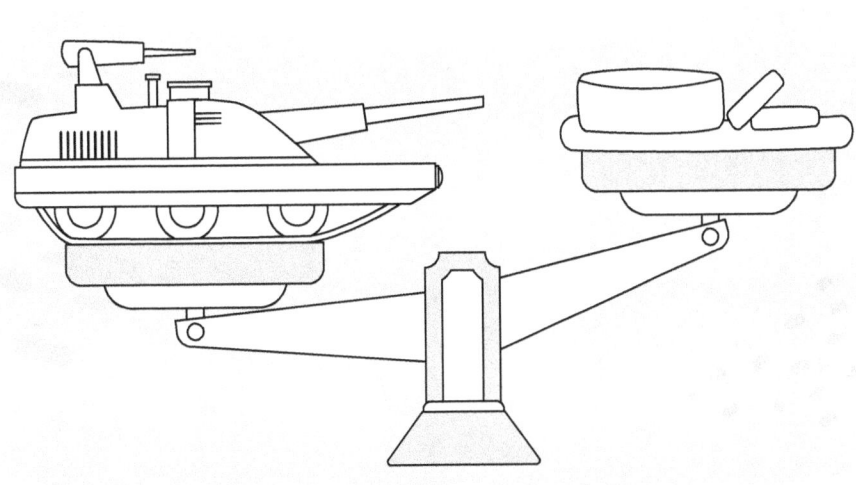

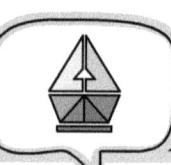
Directions: Read the text below. Then answer the questions that follow.

This week you learned about the Vietnam War, the reaction to it, and the ways in which the war undermined domestic programs in the United States.

1. Elaborate on how the legislation of the Great Society was related to the legislation of the New Deal.

2. Which Great Society program do you view as being the most important? Why?

3. In what ways has the counterculture of the Vietnam War era influenced culture today? Provide examples.

4. In your view, was the United States justified in sending troops to Vietnam? Elaborate on your reasoning.

WEEK 18

Economics

America in the 70s

This week, you will learn about the economic problems of the 1970s, including the oil shocks of the period leading to the election of Ronald Reagan in 1980.

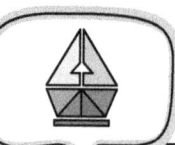
Directions: Read the text below. Then answer the questions that follow.

In the 1970s, the United States ended its long period of post-war economic expansion. The first major shock to the economy occurred from 1973 to 1975, brought on by spikes in oil prices and spending on the Vietnam War.

The spikes in oil prices were called **oil shocks** and occurred first in 1973 and then 1979. The cause of the 1973 shock was the decision by Arab members of the **Organization of Petroleum Exporting Companies** (OPEC) to **embargo**, or block, the sale of oil to the United States and other countries due to American support for Israel in the 1973 Arab-Israeli War. These members of OPEC also cut oil production.

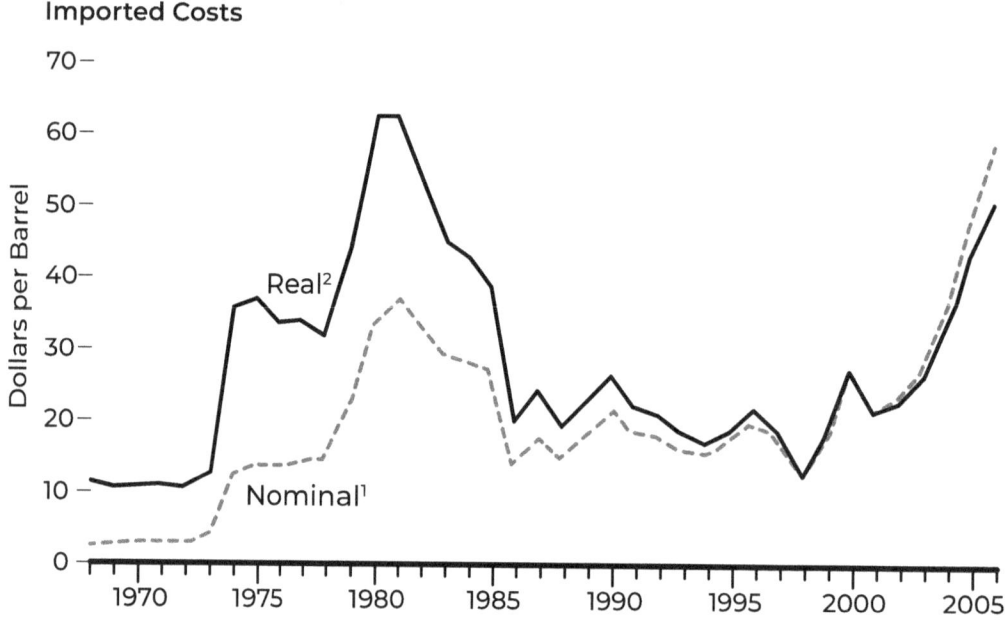

Since demand for oil remained the same, the lower supply resulted in higher oil prices. In the United States, long lines at the gas stations were common. It was only when a truce was arranged in 1974 that the embargo was lifted.

The second shock occurred during the Iranian Revolution. Iran was a major oil producer, so again oil shortages resulted, and within a year, prices doubled.

The oil shocks showed the impact of **globalization** on the United States, as the economies of different countries were more tightly bound together. It also showed how the United States had become highly dependent on importing oil from overseas.

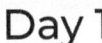

1. Which of the following would be an example of an embargo?

    A. the United States banning oil imports to develop its own industry

    B. the United States refusing to sell automobiles to another country for political reasons

    C. the United States reducing output of computers in order to control prices

    D. the United States brokering a trade deal to open markets with another country

2. For what reason did OPEC start the 1973 oil shock?

    A. It was protesting the United States' support for Israel.

    B. It was supporting the revolutionary government in Iran.

    C. It was trying to increase profits for member nations such as Iran.

    D. It was using its trade leverage to open new oil markets in North America.

3. Why did OPEC's actions in 1973 lead to increased oil prices?

    A. Demand for oil decreased and supply decreased.

    B. Demand for oil increased as supply remained the same.

    C. Demand for oil remained the same but supply decreased.

    D. Demand for oil was flat and supply was flat.

4. According to the graph, in about what year did the price of oil peak?

    A. 1980

    B. 1973

    C. 1986

    D. 1975

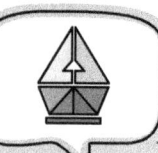
Directions: Read the text below. Then answer the questions that follow.

One of the problems with the economy of the 1970s into the early 1980s was **inflation**. Inflation in economics is the natural rise in prices. For example, a comic book in the 1960s may have sold for ten cents while today a copy of the latest comic book may sell for several dollars. Some inflation is normal, since as people spend money, sellers will gradually increase their prices. Inflation is often bearable for citizens because wages usually increase as well. Economies could tolerate some inflation as long as people were employed.

During the 1970s, however, the United States suffered severe inflation from the oil shocks. Inflation did not just impact the price of oil but also impacted the price of everything. Meanwhile, unemployment remained high and economic growth was slow. Economists called this **stagflation**.

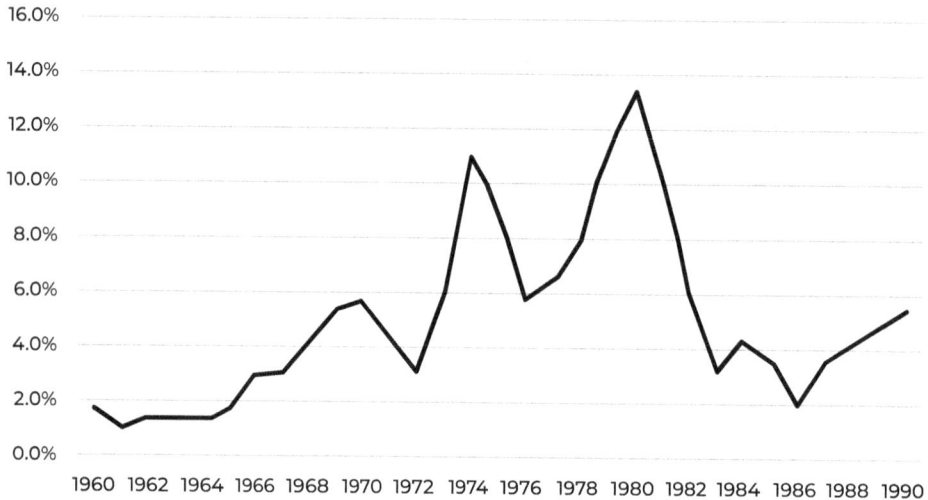

United States Inflation Rate, 1960-1990

It was not until the 1980s that inflation came under control and economic growth resumed. This was credited to the **Federal Reserve,** which managed monetary policy in the United States. In order to slow inflation, the Federal Reserve dramatically increased interest rates. This increased loan rates so that people paid much more to borrow money for houses and other large items. This change had the effect of slowing down the economy, which entered into a recession in the early 1980s. It also stopped inflation, and eventually the economy recovered.

1. What is the difference between inflation and stagflation?

....

....

....

2. What did the Federal Reserve do to control inflation?

    A. raised interest rates on loans

    B. lowered interest rates on loans

    C. issued more loans

    D. reduced the number of loans

3. According to the graph, in about what year was inflation at its highest?

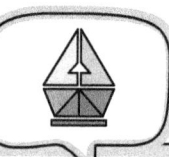
Directions: Read the text below. Then answer the questions that follow.

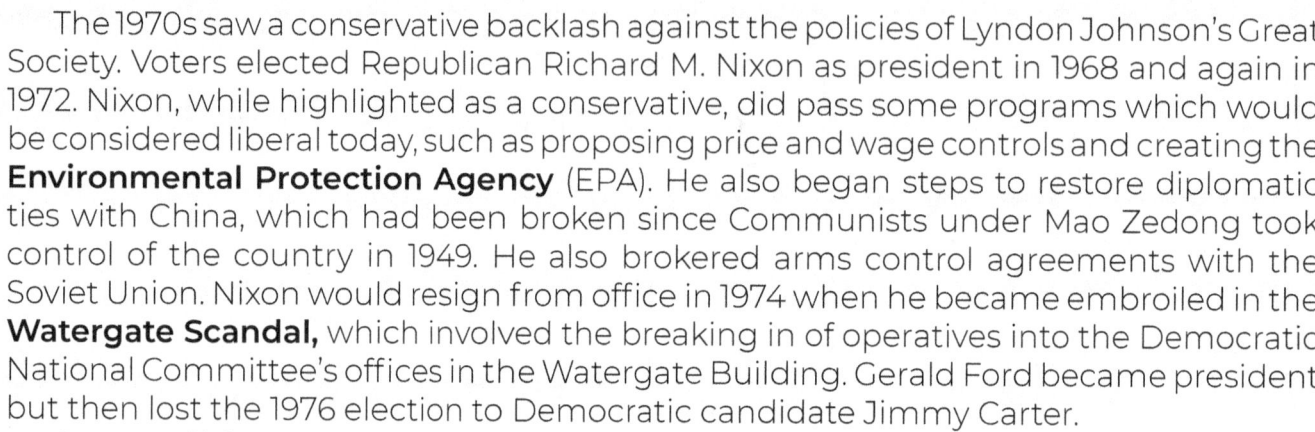

The 1970s saw a conservative backlash against the policies of Lyndon Johnson's Great Society. Voters elected Republican Richard M. Nixon as president in 1968 and again in 1972. Nixon, while highlighted as a conservative, did pass some programs which would be considered liberal today, such as proposing price and wage controls and creating the **Environmental Protection Agency** (EPA). He also began steps to restore diplomatic ties with China, which had been broken since Communists under Mao Zedong took control of the country in 1949. He also brokered arms control agreements with the Soviet Union. Nixon would resign from office in 1974 when he became embroiled in the **Watergate Scandal,** which involved the breaking in of operatives into the Democratic National Committee's offices in the Watergate Building. Gerald Ford became president but then lost the 1976 election to Democratic candidate Jimmy Carter.

Carter still faced the problems of a poor economy. At the end of his term, he was faced with the **Iran Hostage Crisis** in which 52 American diplomats and citizens were held hostage by the revolutionary government in Iran. This issue continued for over a year. The mood of the country generally darkened amongst economic downturn and political scandal. Carter noted that the country lacked "confidence and a sense of community." In the election of 1980, Republican candidate Ronald Reagan won in a landslide victory against Carter. Reagan worked to reduce the size of the federal government, viewing it as too intrusive in people's lives.

1. From the passage above, explain why Carter said that the United States lacked "confidence and a sense of community."

....

....

....

2. From the passage above, explain how Nixon's administration may be viewed by some as having a mixed record.

....

....

....

....

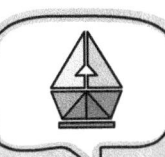
Directions: Read the text below. Then answer the questions that follow.

66

The following passage is an excerpt from President Ronald Reagan's first inaugural address on January 20, 1981:

"It is no coincidence that our present troubles parallel and are proportionate to the intervention and intrusion in our lives that result from unnecessary and excessive growth of government. It is time for us to realize that we are too great a nation to limit ourselves to small dreams. We are not, as some would have us believe, doomed to an inevitable decline. I do not believe in a fate that will fall on us no matter what we do. I do believe in a fate that will fall on us if we do nothing. So, with all the creative energy at our command, let us begin an era of national renewal. Let us renew our determination, our courage, and our strength. And let us renew our faith and our hope."

99

1. Based on the passage, what do you think Reagan's attitude was towards the Great Society?

....

....

....

....

2. Based on your previous readings, how does Reagan's speech capture the national mood of his time? What is the mood of his speech?

....

....

....

....

....

....

....

....

....

99

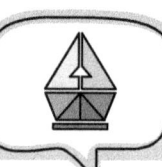
Directions: Read the text below. Then answer the questions that follow.

This week you learned about the 1970s and some of the economic problems of the era. You also learned about other problems from the period that eventually led to the election of Ronald Reagan as president in 1980.

1. Elaborate on how stagflation harmed the economy during the 1970s. How would stagflation impact working families?

_____

_____

_____

_____

2. What was the difference in tone between Jimmy Carter and Ronald Reagan? Why was this important?

_____

_____

_____

_____

3. How did the oil shocks of the 1970s demonstrate globalization?

_____

_____

_____

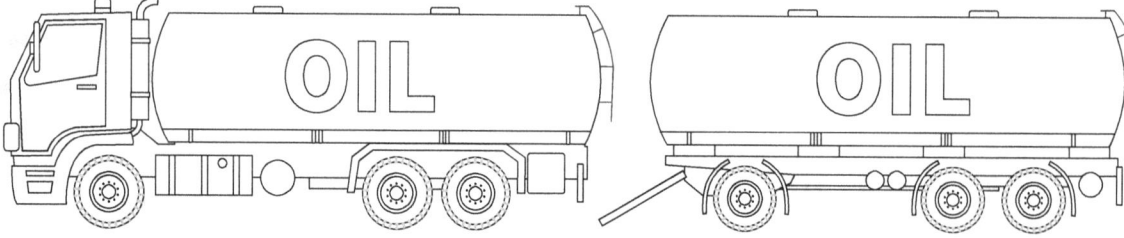

WEEK 19

History

The End of the Cold War

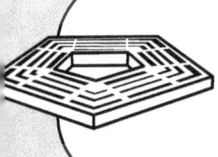

This week, you will learn about the end of the Cold War and the issues that came after it leading up to the September 11, 2001 terrorist attacks.

ARGOPREP

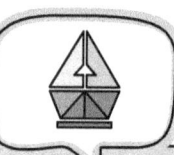
Directions: Read the text below. Then answer the questions that follow.

In the 1980s, Ronald Reagan used rhetoric which inflamed the Cold War. He referred to the Soviet Union as an "**evil empire.**" He also called upon the head of the Soviet Union **Mikhael Gorbachev** to tear down the Berlin Wall. The wall, which had been constructed in 1961, stood as a symbol between the democratic West Berlin and the totalitarian East Berlin. However, by the end of the Reagan administration, tensions had cooled, and the United States signed nuclear arms control treaties.

By the end of the 1980s, there were problems in the Soviet Union. The **command economy** system in which the government planned out all economic moves in the country was inefficient and began to collapse. In contrast, the United States had a **free market economy** where economic decisions were made by the people based on their demand and the supply of goods.

Some believe the collapse of the Soviet Union was sped up when Reagan escalated the Cold War and forced the Soviet Union to spend more on its military spending. To try to revive the Soviet Union, Gorbachev instituted polices of *glasnost* (encouraging a more transparent government and wider dissemination of information) and *perestroika* (reforming the economic and political system). While the regime remained authoritarian, these policies were meant to open the Soviet Union to western ideas and start adopting a small capitalistic market system. These freedoms seemed to inspire those countries that had been dominated by the Soviet Union since the end of World War II to push for their own freedom. In 1989, these countries elected non-communist governments. Gorbachev, unlike prior Soviet leaders, refused to send in the military. The Berlin Wall was torn down, and Germany was reunified in 1990. One at a time, the communist states of Eastern Europe and the Soviet Union collapsed. By 1991, the Cold War was over.

1. How was Mikhail Gorbachev different from previous leaders of the Soviet Union?
   A. He tried to open the country to western ideas.
   B. He adopted large scale economic changes based on capitalism.
   C. He used the military to quash resistance.
   D. He established a democratic constitution in the Soviet Union.

2. What was a probable outcome of the increase in tensions in the early 1980s between the Soviet Union and the United States?
   A. The Soviet economy could not keep up with the American economy.
   B. The two superpowers signed a nuclear arms reduction treaty.
   C. The Berlin Wall was torn down.
   D. The Soviet Union instituted reforms.

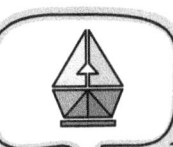
3. Why would spending more on the military lead to the Soviet Union's economic collapse?

    A. The Soviet Union's satellite countries put too much of a strain on its economy.

    B. The Soviet Union's military used the funding to escalate the Cold War.

    C. The Soviet Union's market economy was unsuitable for military spending.

    D. The Soviet Union's economy could not handle the additional expenditures.

4. What is a command economy?

    A. an economy where all decisions are made by the military

    B. an economy where all decisions are made by the government

    C. an economy where all decisions are made by laws of supply and demand

    D. an economy where all decisions are made by the people

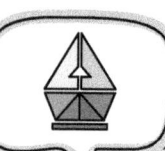
Directions: Read the text below. Then answer the questions that follow.

George H.W. Bush was president of the United States at the end of the Cold War. In the last days of the Soviet Union, he negotiated a new arms-reduction treaty with Mikhail Gorbachev. He also pushed for the reunification of Germany. Bush was surprised when the Soviet Union collapsed in 1991 and cautiously established diplomatic relations with new governments that emerged from the wreck of the Soviet state.

At the same time, the United States became directly involved in the Middle East with the Persian Gulf War. This war was caused when Iraq, led by its dictator Saddam Hussein, invaded its neighboring country, Kuwait. The United States gathered a coalition of forces from 35 other countries from 1990 to 1991. The Soviet Union maintained neutrality as the coalition drove Iraq out of Kuwait. As Iraqi forces retreated, they set uncontrollable fires to Kuwaiti oil wells. The fires burned for ten months, causing extensive environmental damage before they were put out.

A peace was brokered, and Hussein remained in power. Bush was criticized for this move, as many argued that he should have removed Hussein from power.

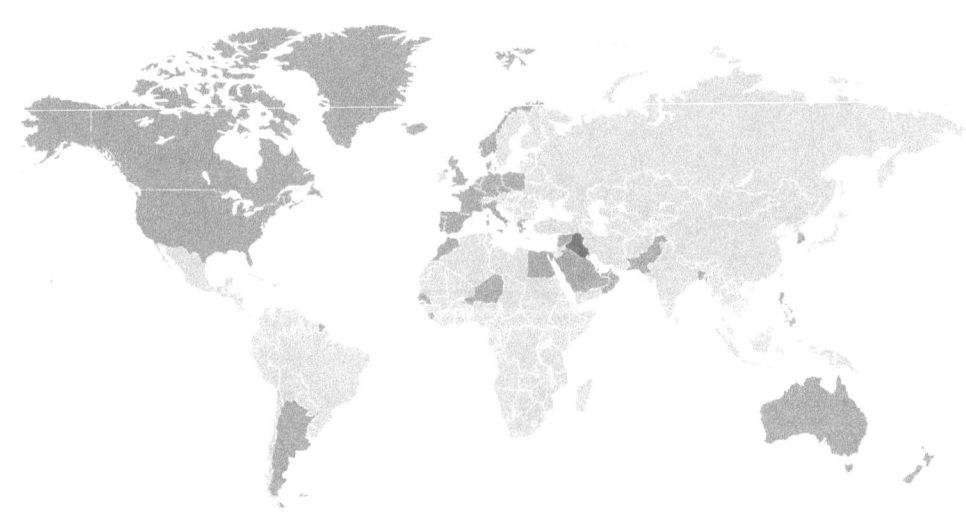

Countries that deployed forces as part of the coalition against Iraq.

1. Why would the Soviet Union have remained neutral during the Persian Gulf War when it had intervened in other wars during the Cold War?

....

....

....

....

2. What does the map say about the nature of the coalition forces during the Persian Gulf War?

....

....

....

....

3. What may have been a reason that the United States did not remove Saddam Hussein from power?

....

....

....

....

4. Considering that the world had two superpowers during the Cold War, what would be the impact of the collapse of the Soviet Union on the United States?

....

....

....

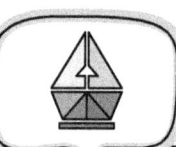
Directions: Read the text below. Then answer the questions that follow.

The end of the Cold War brought changes to borders and government in the Soviet Union and Eastern Europe. These two maps illustrate those changes.

Cold War Military alliances

- Founding members of the North Atlantic Alliance (NATO) 1949
- Entry: Greece and Turkey 1952, West Germany 1955, Spain 1982
- Founding members of the Warsaw Pact 1955
- Entry: East Germany 1956
- Withdrawal: Albania 1968

Iceland

Sweden

Finland

Norway

Denmark

Ireland

United Kingdom

Netherlands

East Germany

Poland

Soviet Union

Belgium

West Germany

Czechoslovakia

Liecht.

Switzerland

Austria

Hungary

France

Romania

Italy

Yugoslavia

Bulgaria

Portugal

Spain

Albania

Greece

Turkey

Morocco

Algeria

Tunisia

Cyprus

Libya

Egypt

Map of Europe in 1990

The End of the Cold War

EXPLAINING THE TOPIC

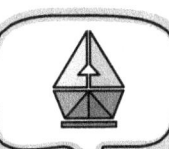

Iceland
Sweden
Finland
Norway
Estonia
Russian Federation
Latvia
Denmark
Lithuania
Russia
Belarus
Ireland
United Kingdom
Nether-lands
Germany
Poland
Belgium
Czech Republic
Liecht.
Ukraine
Slovakia
Moldova
Switzer-land
Austria
Hungary
France
Slovenia
Croatia
Romania
Italy
Bosnia and Herzegovina
Serbia
Bulgaria
Georgia
Montenegro
Macedonia
Albania
Portugal
Spain
Greece
Turkey
Tunisia
Cyprus
Algeria
Morocco
Libya
Egypt

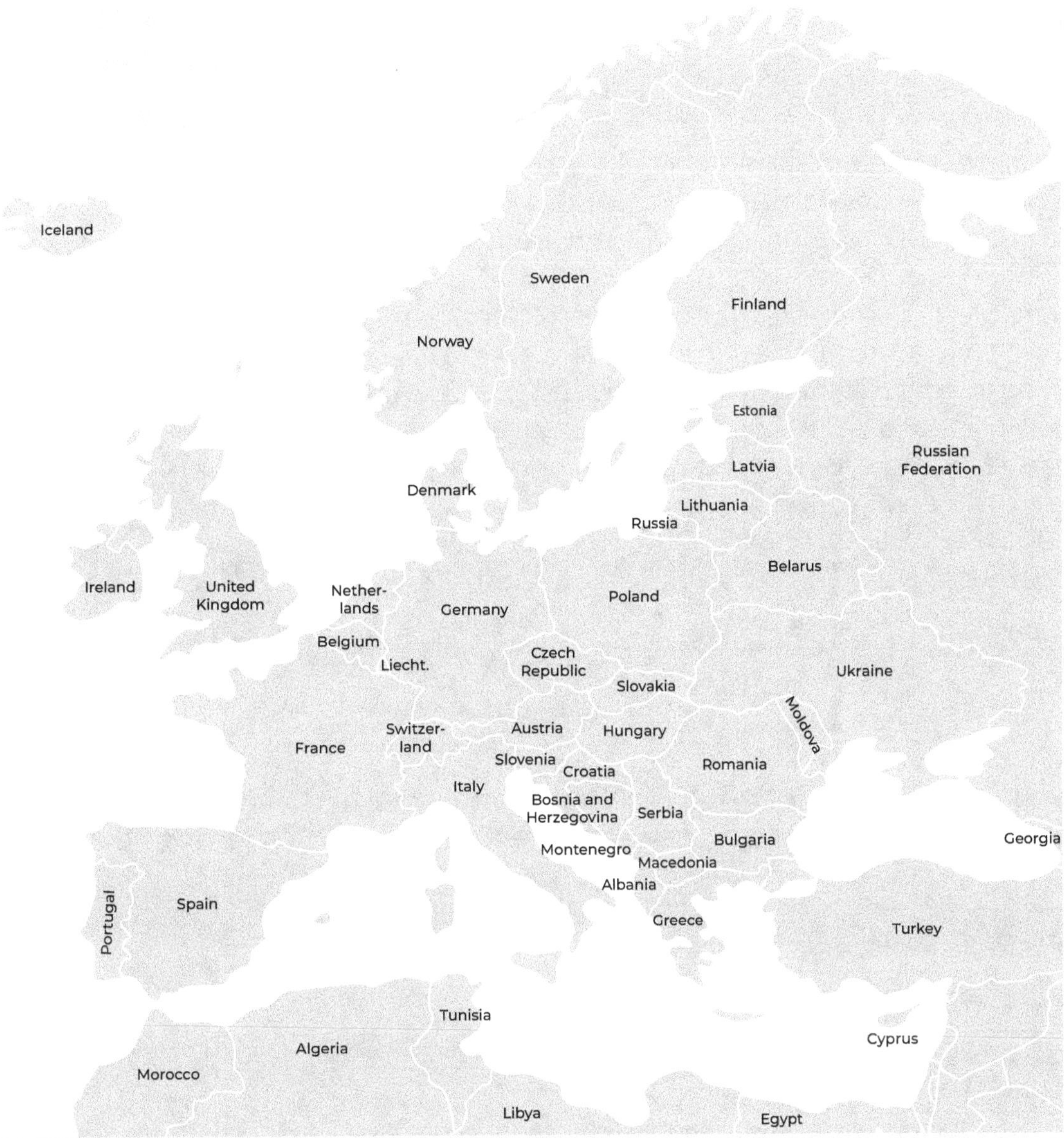

1. Which countries that are in Eastern Europe today were parts of the Soviet Union?

....

....

2. What is different about Germany between the Cold War and today?

....

....

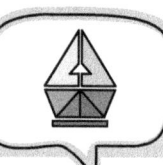
Directions: Read the text below. Then answer the questions that follow.

With the Cold War over, the United States became the world's only superpower. In that position, the United States was able to push for its own policy goals around the world. However, the world itself was changing and international conflicts were becoming more complex. This was coupled with a rise in terrorism. Groups felt the United States had become too powerful and was inserting itself into other countries' matters. This culminated in attacks by the organization **Al-Qaeda** which destroyed the World Trade Center in New York City and damaged the Pentagon on September 11, 2001. In total, 2,977 people died during these attacks, and September 11 became a moment which many Americans will remember for the rest of their lives.

Consider your own experiences. What global events do you remember most in your lifetime? How does that compare to an event like the September 11 attacks?

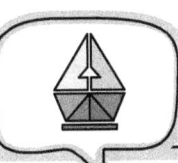
Directions: Read the text below. Then answer the questions that follow.

This week you learned about the end of the Cold War and its impact on the United States leading up to the September 11 terrorist attacks. Consider your reading as you respond to the following questions.

1. In your opinion, is the world more dangerous today than it was during the Cold War? Why or why not?

_____

_____

_____

_____

2. How do the September 11 attacks demonstrate globalism and how are they linked with the end of the Cold War?

_____

_____

_____

_____

3. In what ways was the end of the Cold War positive?

_____

_____

_____

_____

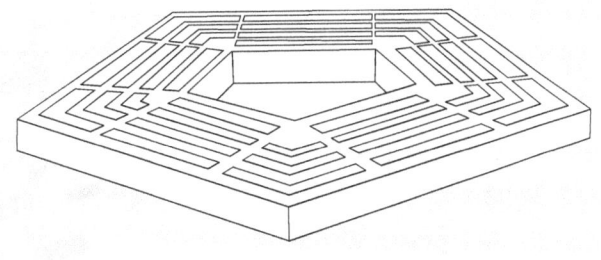

WEEK 20

Economics

America and the Global World

NAFTA

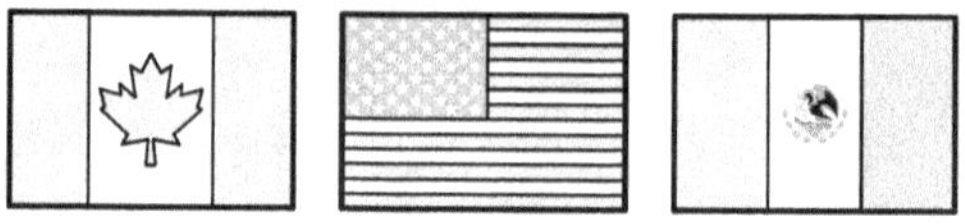

This week, you will learn about the United States' place in a global world as well as the impact of technology on society.

ARGOPREP

Directions: Read the text below. Then answer the questions that follow.

In the beginning of the 21st century the United States has found itself a part of a complex global community that has grown more tightly knit due to advances in technology. At the same time, these technological advances have created new problems that people are debating today.

Economically, the world has become **globalized** and **interdependent**. Interdependence means that the world depends more and more on other countries for goods and materials. For example, the iPhone is very popular in the United States, but it is manufactured in China as well as in other countries around the world. Trade deals, such as the **North American Free Trade Agreement** (NAFTA) or the creation of the **European Union** (EU) have opened up borders worldwide. This has resulted in a reduction or the elimination of tariffs, which are taxes on foreign goods. While such agreements have increased trade and wealth, they have also disrupted conditions for workers in traditional industries. Also, as borders have come down, so too has there been increasing pressure on the United States by people who want to immigrate to it. Immigration, as it has been in the past, is an issue of debate in the country.

As the world has become more closely connected, it has also become more susceptible to acts of terrorism by organizations not representing specific countries. As you learned last week, the most prominent attack on the United States was the September 11, 2001 attacks. Since then, the United States has implemented new policies and departments to combat terrorism, such as the creation of the **Department of Homeland Security** and the passing of the **USA Patriot Act,** which has given the government more latitude in surveillance. The United States has also become more directly involved by attacking suspected terrorist locations.

1. What is an example of economic interdependence?
   A. Japanese factories making automobiles bought in the United States.
   B. American farms in Iowa growing crops sold in New York.
   C. New taxes on imported goods from China.
   D. Sports teams in a league playing in Canada and the United States.

2. How can open borders help generate wealth?
   A. They allow goods made in one country to be easily sold in another.
   B. They allow goods made in one country to be easily taxed by another.
   C. They allow goods to be made more efficiently.
   D. They allow for the free movement of ideas.

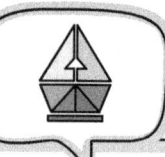
3. What is a tariff?

    A. an agreement that opens borders

    B. a tax on an imported good

    C. a treaty regarding immigration

    D. a company headquartered in a foreign country

4. What did the USA Patriot Act allow the government to do?

    A. regulate the Internet

    B. open borders

    C. create tariffs

    D. more easily monitor people

European Union

China

United States
of America

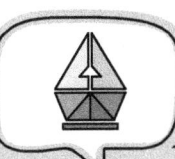
Directions: Read the text below. Then answer the questions that follow.

The North American Free Trade Agreement (NAFTA) was signed into law by President Bill Clinton in 1993 and went into effect in 1994. NAFTA eliminated most trade restrictions between the United States, Canada, and Mexico. It also reduced the restriction of movement of people between these borders. Since its inauguration, trade has increased tremendously.

NAFTA was hotly debated at the time of its approval. Supporters contended that it would increase wealth and promote general prosperity. Critics believed that NAFTA would make it harder for workers to organize since jobs could now move more easily overseas which, they argued, would result in lower wages.

The results of NAFTA have been mixed. There has been an increase in the gross domestic product and trade between the three countries. There has also been a growing interdependency. Experts believe that NAFTA will result in further cooperation between the countries. However, there have indeed been job losses in the manufacturing sector, especially among high paying manufacturing jobs. Since labor is cheaper in Mexico, some jobs have migrated there. There have also been job gains. It is unclear, however, if both of these were due to NAFTA.

President Donald Trump was a critic of NAFTA, and after taking office in 2016 forced a new negotiation. His decision resulted in the **United States-Canada-Mexico Agreement** (USMCA) which was ratified in 2020 and took effect on July 1 of that year. This agreement replaced NAFTA. The USMCA is a similar agreement but strengthens labor standards with one provision stating that up to 45 percent of parts for a vehicle must come from a factory that pays workers a minimum of $16 an hour in order to become tariff free. There is also more focus on automobile production in North America which was meant to boost growth in the automobile industry. The impact of USMCA remains to be seen.

NAFTA
The North American Free Trade Agreement

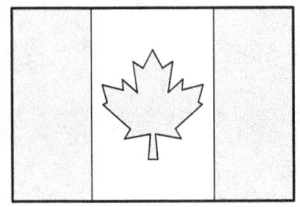

Canada

United States
of America

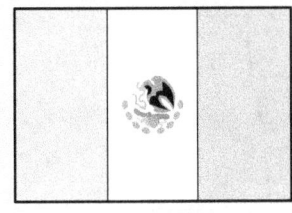

Mexico

1. What is an objective of both NAFTA and USMCA?
    A. to strengthen the manufacturing industry
    B. to increase trade across member countries
    C. to expand the number of member countries
    D. to enhance labor standards

2. What is a benefit of an agreement like NAFTA or USMCA?

....

....

....

3. How could agreements that lower restrictions on trade hurt organized labor?

....

....

....

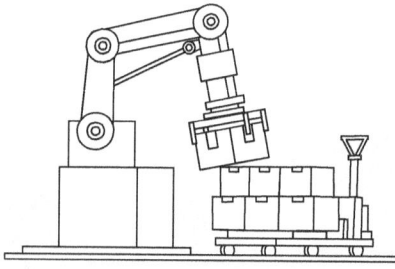

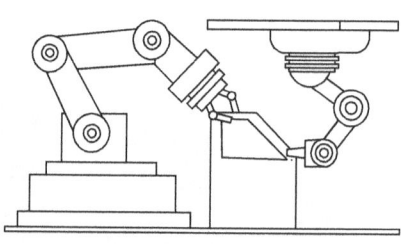

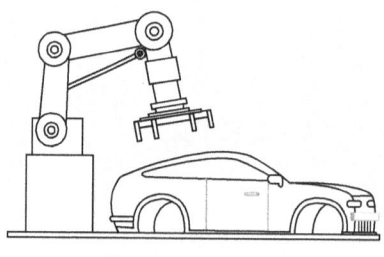

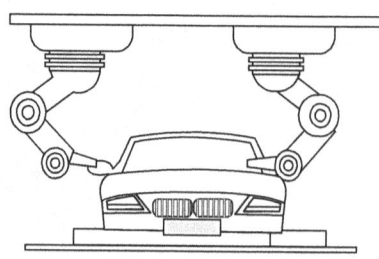

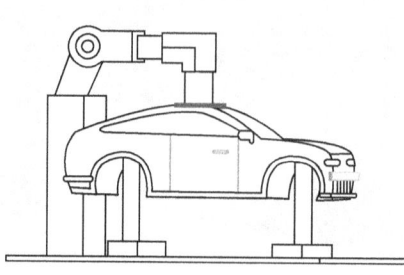

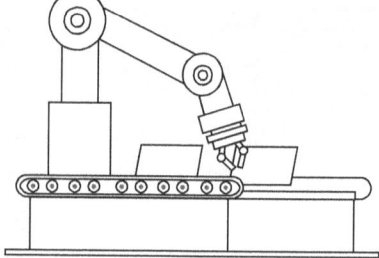

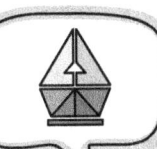
Directions: Read the text below. Then answer the questions that follow.

Immigration into the United States is a subject of debate. In the 1920s, anti-immigrant sentiment led Congress to enact a quota system on immigration based on national origin. This system was biased toward those of Western European origin and was ended in 1965.

Since then, immigration has increased with immigrants coming from a more diverse number of areas than they did in the 19th and early 20th centuries.

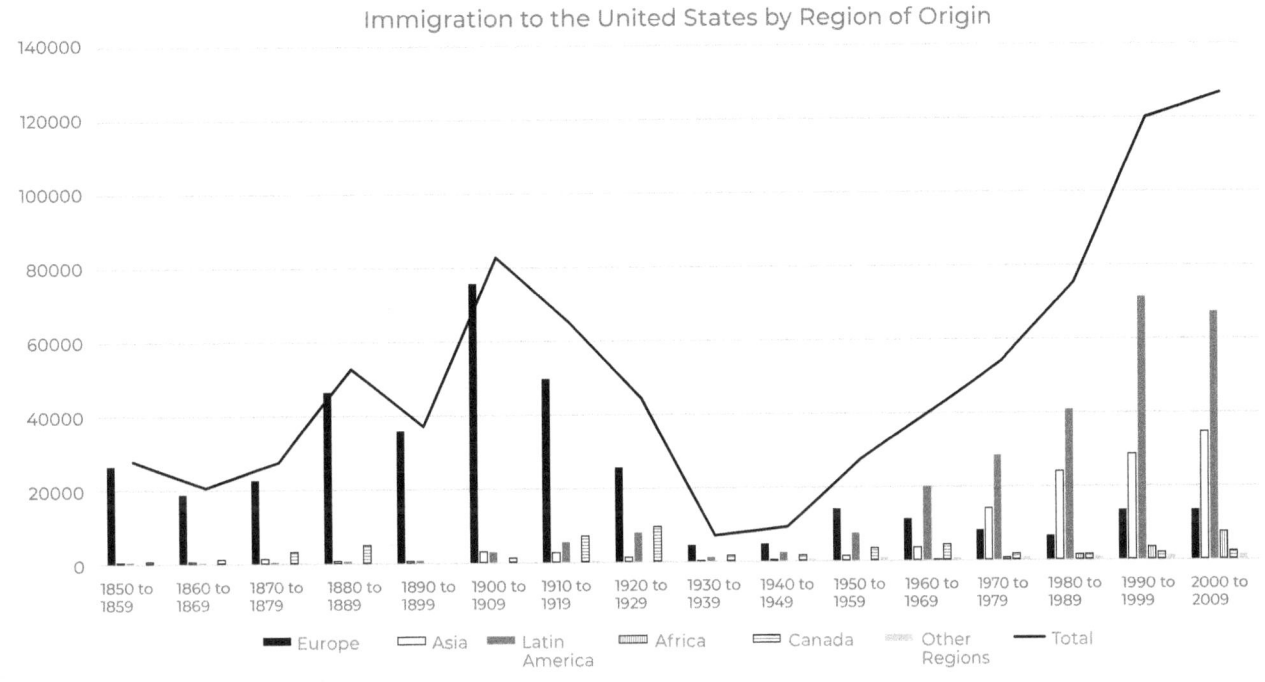

Immigration to the United States by Region of Origin

1. Explain what the graph says has been the trend in immigration to the United States since 1965.

   ....

   ....

2. Explain how the immigration of today is different from the immigration of a century ago.

   ....

   ....

Directions: Read the text below. Then answer the questions that follow.

"

After the September 11 attacks, Congress passed the USA Patriot Act which stands for Uniting and Strengthening America by Providing Appropriate Tools Required to Intercept and Obstruct Terrorism. This act was designed to give the government more power to investigate, prevent, and punish people committing acts of terrorism. Supporters argue that these powers allows the FBI to stop terrorist plots before they occur. Critics state that the Patriot Act violates people's rights since it allows the government to monitor and study them without due process of law.

"

1. What are the benefits of the USA Patriot Act?

....
....
....
....

2. What is your stance on the Patriot Act?

....
....
....
....

3. Based on your response above, draw a political cartoon to illustrate your opinion.

Directions: Read the text below. Then answer the questions that follow.

"
This week you learned about how the United States has become part of a global community, and how being part of that community has created new challenges.

The following quote is an excerpt from a speech delivered by President Barack Obama on May 29, 2009:

It's the great irony of our Information Age - the very technologies that empower us to create and to build also empower those who would disrupt and destroy. And this paradox - seen and unseen - is something that we experience every day.
"

1. How have advances in communication technology created a more connected world?

_____

_____

_____

_____

2. What is the paradox President Obama is referring to?

_____

_____

_____

_____

3. List three technological items you possess that you would not give up. What would be the impact of losing those items?

_____

_____

_____

_____

_____

_____

Answer Sheets

To see the answer key to the entire workbook, you can easily download the answer key from our website!

*Due to the high request from parents and teachers, we have removed the answer key from the workbook so you do not need to rip out the answer key while students work on the workbook.

To watch free video explanations go to: **argoprep.com/social8**
OR scan the QR Code:

Place your mouse over the workbook you have, and you will see the "Download Answers" button.

For detailed video instructions on how to access the "Answer Sheets," please scan this QR code.

Books explanations

All Books   Grade: **All**   ⌄   Series: **Social Studies**   ⌄   🔍 Search...

7th Grade Social Studies: Daily Practice Workbook

5th Grade Social Studies: Daily Practice Workbook

8th Grade Social Studies: Daily Practice Workbook

4th Grade Social Studies: Daily Practice Workbook

3rd Grade Social Studies: Daily Practice Workbook

8th Grade Social Studies: Daily

⬇ Download Answers

4th Grade Social Studies: Practice Workbook